C B Berry

The Other Side

C B Berry

The Other Side

ISBN/EAN: 9783744659727

Printed in Europe, USA, Canada, Australia, Japan

Cover: Foto ©Thomas Meinert / pixelio.de

More available books at **www.hansebooks.com**

Eric Gordon.

THE OTHER SIDE,

HOW IT STRUCK US.

THE OTHER SIDE

HOW IT STRUCK US

BY

C. B. BERRY

GRIFFITH AND FARRAN
Successors to Newbery and Harris
WEST CORNER OF ST PAUL'S CHURCHYARD, LONDON
E. P. DUTTON & CO., NEW YORK.
1880.

The rights of translation and of reproduction are reserved.

CONTENTS

	PAGE
CHAPTER I.	
OUTWARD BOUND	1
CHAPTER II.	
AMERICAN HOTELS	14
CHAPTER III.	
NEW YORK	27
CHAPTER IV.	
AMERICAN RAILWAYS . . .	39
CHAPTER V.	
THE QUAKER CITY	57
CHAPTER VI.	
"THE CITY OF MAGNIFICENT DISTANCES"	68

CONTENTS.

PAGE

CHAPTER VII.
RICHMOND 88

CHAPTER VIII.
A LONG JOURNEY, AND A SQUALLING BABY . 100

CHAPTER IX.
SOMETHING ABOUT CHICAGO . . 111

CHAPTER X.
SOMETHING MORE ABOUT CHICAGO . . 124

CHAPTER XI.
A PRAIRIE VILLAGE . . . 137

CHAPTER XII.
DETROIT AND NIAGARA . . . 162

CHAPTER XIII.
THE QUEEN CITY OF THE WEST . . 184

CHAPTER XIV.
TO THE WOODS 198

CHAPTER XV.
THE CANADIAN BUSH . . . 214

CHAPTER XVI.
THE BAY OF QUINTE, AND THE STONE CITY . 233

CHAPTER XVII.

OTTAWA 246

CHAPTER XVIII.

MONTREAL AND QUEBEC . . . 261

CHAPTER XIX.

THE LEARNED CITY 274

CHAPTER XX.

EASTWARDS AWAY 284

THE OTHER SIDE:
HOW IT STRUCK US.

CHAPTER I.

OUTWARD BOUND.

IT was a fine frosty November evening, as my friend Davis and I stood on the Prince's Pier landing-stage, Greenock, waiting to embark on the steamer that was to carry us to the New World. We had bidden a temporary, though hardly reluctant, farewell to the fascinations of commerce, and were prepared to employ a six months' furlough in visiting America;—revelling, like schoolboys released, in the prospect of a period unbroken by grim calculations of "profit and loss," and totally unshadowed by such a thing as a business letter.

Half-an-hour, and we stood upon the big ship's deck, and saw the tender vanish shorewards into the night, severing by its departure the last link that connected us with the land of our birth. Then

Westward Ho! and away,—for the home of brother Jonathan!

The voyage was not remarkable: we had no startling incident of storm or peril; but the days slid by in a lazy, luxurious monotony. We paced the deck, or reclined comfortably under the lee of the deck-houses, looking out over the expanse of waters—ever the same, and yet always changing—the wave-crests curling to every swell of the breeze, and sinking again as it died; the broad bosom of the ocean now dull beneath a leaden cloudbank, now bathed in the blood-red glow of the setting sun, and giving back its splendour from the long "send" of each great Atlantic billow. But intellectual pursuits were not altogether neglected: there were books and chess in the saloon and smoking-room; and hardly an hour passed in which some industrious quartette might not be seen busy at whist; while, with a proper regard to contingencies in the land of the free to which we were bound, Davis and I endeavoured, with the able assistance of an experienced fellow-passenger, to gain some insight into "euchre" and "poker."

Our companions presented considerable opportunity for the study of character. We had a gentleman from Chicago, whose stories of the Western "porkopolis" were awe-inspiring; a Scotchman from a prairie town; a Canadian with a talent (or at least a fondness) for argument; and a Yankee from the New England States, whose performances at table capped the whole. This attractive individual seemed to regard his meals—as indeed everything else—in a strictly commercial light: he proved to be on his way back from "doing Eu*rope*" on an £80 tourist ticket, and had evidently made up his mind to have, in everything, the utmost value for his money.

The Chicago man thought that there was no place on earth like Chicago, and was always eager to launch into descriptions. He was inclined to become somewhat extravagant in its praises; and conversations like the following were of daily occurrence:—

(Chicago man—nasally): "Chicago, sir, is the most *re*markable city of the day. You just start around and *pro*spect, and see where you can find its living equal for progress. We go ahead, sir, in Chicago. We advance, *I* tell you. We have the tallest produce trade in the world; and I calculate, sir, we turn over more dollars there in one week, than London does in a month."

"How about St. Louis?"

"Saint Louis! (with infinite contempt). I wouldn't be found dead in Saint Louis. Saint Louis ain't a paltry circumstance to Chicago. Only thing Saint

Louis *can* really go ahead in is the plague: they do succeed in fevers there most uncommon."

"Indeed! a most unhappy pre-eminence."

"Yes, sir, I tell you again, Chicago is the boss commercial city of the age. Just look, now, at our m*oo*nicipal instit*oo*tions. Look at our streets. They're spacious, sir, and elegant. Only take the length of them; there's Halsted Street runs for thirty-eight miles in one straight line—"

"All through the city?"

"Why no, I guess hardly. You see it extends on to the prairie a bit. But we're rapidly building outwards."

"Ah! then your idea in the West is to lay out your streets first, and build up to them?"

"That's where it is, sir. That's progress,—that's enterprise. Then look at our buildings. Our dry goods stores are the finest in existence, solid, sir, *and* ornamental, with seven floors and steam elevators. Our public instit*oo*tions are in the newest known style of architecture (!) Yes *sir*, I remark that our buildings are without a parallel."

"So, I presume, are your fire engines?"

(Chicago man, entirely ignoring the hit, but catching at the new idea). "Now, I just guess you have struck it. Our fire system is the most wonderful known. It's entirely perfect. You mean to visit Chicago, sir, I think you said?"

"I have every intention of doing so.

"Then you'll see it in operation, and judge for yourself." (I did see it in operation almost every day of my stay in Chicago).

"You have heard of our Stock Yards, I guess?"

"I have, more than once."

"Well, sir, they'll surprise you. I may say they'll strike you considerably. They're the most extraordin*air*ily expansive enclosures in America. They run the cattle right into the yards on the cars, kill them, cut them up, salt them, and pack them, before you can open your mouth to say they are smart. Ah! you'll recognise when you go to Chicago that we are a sharp people. You'll begin to know then that you are living, you bet your life!"

"Chicago and the Western districts are pretty quiet now, I suppose—person and property well protected now, I fancy?"

"Quite, sir. You are as safe in the streets of Chicago at any hour of the day or night, as in any city in England. Safer indeed. The law is supreme, personal violence unknown. Yes *sirree*, the rights of citizens are firmly secured in Chicago."

"I had the idea that a little pistol practice still

lingered on in the Western States, and that it was not an uncommon thing to carry a pocket companion. You find that unnecessary, however?"

"Well, I do sleep with my revolver by my head; but that's to please my wife, and because I don't care to have loaded firearms laying around loose in the way of the children. And then, you will remark that I live pretty far out, in a new part of the city. Besides—thunder! there's the lunch bell. I guess I'll just adjourn and fix myself a bit."

So we lounged, and chatted, and amused ourselves for ten days, till the New York pilot boat appeared in sight, two hundred miles from land. These boats are so famous for their beauty, weatherly qualities, and the skill with which they are sailed, that a word about them may not be out of place. They are all of the same class, differing only in size; so in describing the one which first met us, I describe them all.

When we caught sight of her five or six miles away to windward, she looked like some beautiful seabird with great white wings, skimming along the horizon. She would have been taken for a yacht, till a closer view revealed a large black number on the mainsail, shewing that she belonged to the pilot fleet. Standing on across our bows till we slowed, she wore, and then, handled like a machine, ran down under our lee, dropping a dingy with two men in it as she passed. Of these two, one was the pilot, who sat in the stern sheets, while the other pulled both oars. The transference of the pilot in so light a skiff is very nice work when a heavy sea is running, but the solitary rower is a man of experience, and brings his tiny craft alongside in masterly style, till a rope is thrown and made fast, and the pilot clambers up the big ship's side. Then back over the Atlantic rollers again to the schooner, which has rounded to under the stern to wait for her boat.

The pilot is a man of imposing presence and dignified self-possession, clad in broad-cloth,—though of a seafaring cut,—with a snowy field of shirt front, and a wide-awake hat. But though thus particular in his attire, he bears on his face the mark of his profession, and his weather-beaten cheeks tell of many a hard battle with the elements. He is met by our captain, and conducted down to luncheon in the saloon, as becoming so important a personage, where he addresses himself to the good things with a true sea appetite. He is a gentleman at large till his duty begins, which is not until we reach Sandy Hook; so when the ceremony of lunch is over he proceeds to the smoking-room, and instals himself with great dignity in the best corner, in charge of a six-inch cigar. And after this has been duly lighted and screwed into his mouth, you may venture to speak to him, as I did.

"That schooner of yours is a tidy little craft," I remarked.

"Yes," he assented, rather pleased; "there ain't much amiss about her."

"What a great press of sail you carry!"

"Why yes; we want to cram on a lot o' canvas when we're racing."

"Racing! When do you race?"

"Why, when there's two of us sight a ship at once, we crowd sail to get down first. We have some mighty excitin' races 'times."

"And does the ship always take the pilot that reaches her first?"

"I guess so; there ain't any difference."

"What is the tonnage, now, of your schooner?"

"A trifle inside o' fifty. We have a lot of room on board."

"And how many pilots do you carry?"

"We leave the port o' Noo York with five pilots and six of a working crew; then, you see, we cruise about, and lay off and on, till the pilots are all taken off by ships. When the last pilot goes off, the schooner runs back to port, takes us aboard again, and off once more."

"How long has the schooner generally to cruise till she gets quit of all her pilots?"

"Why, it's all uncertain. Sometimes she'll have good luck and be able to run home in a week; then, again, if ships be scarce, she'll stop out till the larder's empty—a month, may be."

"That is a long time to wait."

"Competition is mighty brisk, and there are twenty-nine certified pilot boats in the port of Noo York. In the summer months you'll see us running five hundred miles off the land, to be the first in the track of the incoming ships."

"Five hundred miles—you don't say so!"

"It's a good thing to be the first to catch an inward ship, for, you see, it's the custom for the same pilot that takes a ship in to take her out again when she leaves."

"Indeed? And how do you arrange about taking ships outward? What if your schooner is cruising at sea with all her pilots when the ship is ready to leave port?"

"Why, the senior pilot belonging to each boat lives on shore always, and goes down the river with all outgoing ships. The vessel drops him at Sandy Hook, so he's back in Noo York city same day."

"Then there are six pilots connected with each

schooner—five on board, and one permanently on shore?"

"I guess that's 'bout how it is."

"And what is the pilotage fee?"

"Five dollars a foot for every foot the ship or steamer draws."

"Then the larger and more deeply-laden the vessel, the better for the pilot."

"Nat'rally."

"You must have some very heavy weather at times. How do the schooners behave?"

"We're out at all seasons, but there ain't cleverer craft anywhere in a gale o' wind or a seaway. Fore-an'-after's are always weatherly; and the pilot boats have both the beam and the depth. You'll seldom hear of an accident to a pilot boat."

"I should think that in fine summer weather you must have rare good times cruising about."

"It's no ways unpleasant. We have an elegant cabin, and always something to read or to amuse us. And gentlemen from the city often come out with us for a holiday."

"Why, that's not at all a bad idea."

"Some o' them are main pleasant company, and perhaps bring down a stock o' wine, and a bit extra for the larder. But they're apt to get sick when it comes on to blow a reg'lar gale o' wind."

During the day the pilot schooner flies a large blue flag at the masthead as a signal, to which the steamer replies if she has not yet got a pilot; and at night she burns a "flare up" whenever she sights a ship's light. Pilotage off the port of New York is a paying business, and many of the pilots retire from sea with a handsome competence.

As we drew nearer the land, coasting craft appeared on all sides, for the most part pretty centre-board schooners, with either two or three masts, and very white sails. Their sails are of cotton, and there is little fog or smoke to blacken them; the absence of smoke being accounted for by the fact that hard coal is used in American cities and steamboats.

The American tug-boats attracted our notice, as essentially different from those at home. They are all screw launches, small and low in the water, but powerful withal. The steersman stands in a glass wheelhouse forward the funnel—the universal plan on all American steamers,—and one which, as protecting that important functionary from wind and sun, is an improvement on our system. Each of those tug-boats bore upon the top of the wheelhouse a large gilt Eagle of Liberty, with outspread wings: and the unhappy birds always appeared to us to be trying hard to escape from the land of the free, as if in protest against some unfitness of the emblem. But they could not make good their flight, for they were tethered by the feet. Luckless eagles of Liberty!

After steaming up fifteen miles through one of the most noble harbours in the world, we reached the quarantine station—Staten Island—where the doctor came on board. His examination was not formidable; and the company being duly passed, we proceeded upwards, marvelling much as we went at the great white unwieldy river steamboats which passed and re-passed all around. Soon we landed at New York City, solemnly swore that we had no " new or dutyable " articles, submitted our effects to inspection by the customs' officer, and then took a cab for the Fifth Avenue Hotel.

The cab merits a word. It was a large and solemn vehicle, eminently suited to any serious occasion, such as a marriage or a funeral, but scarcely adapted for rapid transit through the streets. It was drawn by two horses; and we were charged by the rapacious cabman two dollars and fifty cents, or ten shillings, for the two mile drive. So notably extortionate are cab-fares in New York, and indeed in most American cities, that Americans themselves generally travel in the street cars, which are to be found on any street of consequence. After twenty minutes' jolting, then, over rather ill-paved streets, we duly arrived at the Fifth Avenue Hotel.

CHAPTER II.

AMERICAN HOTELS.

ALIGHTING from our cab at the Fifth Avenue Hotel, we found ourselves in a lofty entrance hall, with a tiled floor — the latter plentifully bedewed with tobacco juice; while the atmosphere was that of a mild Turkish bath, pervaded by a strong odour of cigars. And now to attempt some description of a first-class American hotel.

To begin with, let it be understood that the American hotel is an establishment of quite a different style from the English, as far before the latter as a baronial mansion surpasses a seaside villa. In external appearance certainly, some of our fine hotels are as imposing as the American; but in point of comfort and arrangements there can be no comparison.

The visitor, on entering, goes up to the office in the hall, and inscribes his name and address in the hotel book. The clerk in charge (there are usually two or three) makes a few pleasant remarks on the natural phenomena of the day or other matters, assigns a bedroom, and summons the bedroom porter. There is no subservient bowing and rubbing of hands, no oily smiling; the American clerk has a great deal of self-respect, and shews it, though in an unaffected and easy way.

The porter now leads the way to the hoist—no longer a hoist, but an "elevator"—and ascends with the visitor; the luggage being sent up by a separate elevator. The elevator is an excellent institution; and in some of the best hotels it is beautifully fitted up, and decorated with mirrors and tasteful carving. So complete is it, that I heard of a foreigner in one instance mistaking it for his bed-room, and beginning forthwith to undress!—but this, needless to say, is somewhat unusual.

Arrived at the bedroom floor, you leave the elevator and proceed along a lengthy corridor to your room, while at every turn of the passage you probably see a hand painted on the wall with extended finger, and below it the words—"This way to the fire-escape." Careful provision is made on every floor for such an avenue of safety. The bedroom is not more remarkable than an English apartment, beyond the fact of its being furnished with a spittoon;—for the Yankee often smokes or chews at his toilet. (I think, indeed, that he occasionally goes to bed with his "quid.") If it be desired, a bedroom can be had with a bathroom attached, for the extra charge of a dollar a-day.

After unpacking his belongings, the visitor descends to the dining-hall, for we will suppose him to be hungry. An attendant is in waiting outside the door, who silently receives his hat, and places it amongst a number of others till he shall come out again. This man renders the hat with a polite bow on the diner's exit, and is scarcely ever known to make a mistake, though he may have a hundred hats under his charge at one time. Now there is not much character about a felt hat—there is perhaps no sublunary object possessed of less distinctive individuality; and as the man never used a ticket or number, I once had the curiosity to ask him how he never failed to return the right headpiece. He said it was simply by taking in carefully the owner's face as he passed, and scrutinising the hat! This custom holds throughout the States; and though only a small thing, it seems not unworthy of remark. Surely a man with such a talent for minute observation would be a valuable acquisition to a detective force.

Within the door a head waiter or usher attends, and precedes you with great ceremony to a table. He is a stately personage this, with an imperial flourish of the arm; and commands the whole force of waiters by the elevation of his finger. In a large dining hall like that of the Fifth Avenue Hotel, there are about a hundred waiters, who stand ranged against the wall till summoned as required by this gastronomic centurion. Everything speaks of order and system. The room is full of small tables seated for four or six, to one of which the expectant diner is marshalled. Then advance a waiter, resplendent in a white waistcoat, who fills a glass of iced water, and presents the bill of fare. Iced water is the first thing at every meal, and is set down without order.

The bill of fare is a marvellous literary effort. It is printed afresh every day, for each meal.* The first time you see an American bill of fare, you are overwhelmed, stunned; dishes crowd one upon another in a countless whirl; and not until you hear an American at your elbow order, with unmoved voice, an avalanche of eight or ten different articles, do you pluck up heart and venture to command a modest plate of soup and some roast beef. The waiter, who has been bending an expectant ear in a fatherly way, silently glides off, and is lost to view in a cloud of other black swallow-tails and white waistcoats. Presently he emerges, and places your order before you;—not all heaped upon one or two plates, but with

* See specimens in Appendix.

a dainty little dish for each meat and each vegetable. The American table is very French in the large number of entrées and little dishes; though a man hungering for a solid English meal can amply satisfy his inclination. But we were pleased to find, that the very finest American steak does not compare with the world-famed beefsteak of old England: for if Columbia were to pass us by in this main point of England's glory, it would indeed be "the most unkindest cut of all." And so your dinner goes on, in a soft and noiseless way, to its final ice cream, when you resume your hat and wend your steps downwards to a meditative pipe.

And this pipe will probably evolve from the tangled web of your brain the following conclusions. You will be thoroughly convinced that the Americans know how to cook a dinner, that they know to admiration how to serve a dinner, but—that they do not as yet know how to eat a dinner. For the American is painfully regardless of propriety and sequence in his viands, and his meal is one abortive effort to blend incongruities—and race against time. He eats, to use one of his own expressions, as if there were no hereafter; and then comes to find that there is a hereafter—and that none so remote—in doctor's bills and dyspepsia. He rarely drinks wine or beer during meals, but empties two or three tumblers of iced water: and the effect of constant draughts of ice-cold water between hot meats is not calculated to lessen the injurious effects of over-rapid eating.

The public rooms of the American hotel are spacious, frequently in *suites*, room opening out of room. The furniture is comfortable, and elegant in design, but the colours are sometimes gorgeous to gaudiness. A tendency to loud colours, and a lavish use of white paint on all the "fixings," are the only faults which can be charged against the American hotel in point of taste.

These houses all glory in an apartment of awful magnificence, the mystery of which it is not my intention to penetrate; but it would never do to pass it by, for it is the especial pride, the sort of "pet child" of the Yankee proprietor. This is the bridal chamber. When not in use, it is exhibited to the stranger, who is expected to regard it with a species of reverential awe. The elaborate sumptuousness of this chamber beggars description; but it is so very terrible that I fear it often defeats its own end. To the man crushed by a sense of recent matrimony, the blow inflicted by such solemn state might not impossibly prove final.

American hotels have fine billiard rooms, holding often ten or fifteen tables. The game is much in favour, especially towards evening; and the lover of billiards may see some very fine play. The American game differs from ours, the table being smaller, and without pockets. It is entirely a cannon game, and some beautiful round-the-table strokes may be seen. The balls are larger than our own, and the cues very broad-pointed; but the power of twist and screw attained by the American with his broad cue is very great.

The hotel bar, if not actually in the billiard room, is sure to be in immediate proximity; and this, as a famous national institution, deserves particular mention. It is a long bar, and very handsomely fitted up—"upholstered," as our cousins say; while in the background rise tiers upon tiers of bottles of every shape and size, enlivened by sparkling crystal. Over this vision of Alnaschar there are no presiding goddesses, as at home; their place is filled by male bar-tenders, in snowy jackets. The Yankee has no time for flirtations or soft-whispered nothings across the counter,—his drink is a matter of business, and he approaches it accordingly. There is no poetry in the Yankee soul in this respect. So long as his drink is scientifically mixed, he does not care whether he receives it through the medium of his own sex, or from the fair hand of woman. The American bar at the Paris Exhibition of '78, with its row of smiling barmaids, was a humbug; there are no barmaids in the States. The Yankee does not want them; if there were such, he would be constrained to take off his hat and make a series of polite observations before feeling at liberty to proceed with his libation, for he is very polite to women. And he would be debarred from talking trade or politics, which are his favourite topics.

At the bar, the American fully makes up for his abstinence at meal-time; drinking, smoking, chewing, and expectorating with much freedom and manifest enjoyment. He is as promiscuous in his liquors as in his food; and the compounds which, to use his own elegant phrase, he "puts himself outside of," or "walks around," are very startling. But, however much he may and does injure his internal economy, he is seldom intoxicated. Drunkenness is to be found in the saloons in low parts of the city, but at the high class bars it is very rare.

The American seldom drinks alone, but prefers to share his potations with one, two, or half-a-dozen companions; and many are the keen business transactions concluded during the discussion of a "cocktail" or "John Collins." The "almighty dollar" is never out of the American brain; and the bar and entrance hall of the hotel are the scenes of many a close bargain,—and this not only in the evening—for in the daytime too, these apartments may be seen thronged with busy talkers. The hall of a centrally situated hotel becomes a sort of Exchange during the day for many business men; a custom which the bar proprietor has certainly no cause to regret.

This entrance hall is a great rendezvous. It is not merely a place to pass through, but the peculiarly favoured spot in which to sit and loiter. In hotels of importance it is large, even to magnificence; sometimes square, sometimes oblong, and again in the shape of a rotunda. The floor is laid with marble or coloured tiles; and round the pillars are grouped large armchairs, in convenient proximity to which rise great bell-mouthed spittoons. Expectoration has assumed in the States the dignity of a science, and provision is made at every turn for its due advance and refinement.

Off the entrance hall there open various important establishments. Through one door you enter the barber's shop, which is as necessary to the hotel-going Yankee as a tub to an Englishman; through another you pass to a hatter's and general hosier's; while within a third there is visible a railway ticket office. Nor are these all; for there are yet a book and news stall, (where, by the way, you may purchase theatre tickets), a telegraph office, and a tobacconist's shop, with goodly array of tobacco and cigar boxes. Every means is thus taken to bring within the hotel itself the appliances needed for everyday life, so as to save the visitor trouble. The concentration of all these conveniences is a saving—not only of trouble—but of time; time is money, and to the American money is everything. To make dollars, and to spend them, comprise his creed.

The American system of hotel charges is generally known to be different from ours. Instead of being charged separately for each item, the visitor pays a fixed rate for the day, everything being included. Thus there can be no robbery or extortion, as is too often the case at home; on entering a hotel, you are given to understand clearly what the daily board costs; that sum you pay, and no more. A card, indeed, with full particulars as to charges, hours of meals, &c., is pasted on the inside of every bedroom door.

Three dollars is the customary day's board in first-class houses throughout the States; though in the Fifth Avenue Hotel, New York, you are charged four. There are hotels in most American cities conducted on the European plan of charging; but an adherence to home customs in this respect will generally be found an expensive luxury. It is a good rule, when travelling, to go to those hotels frequented by the natives of the country; for in houses both on the continent and in the United States, which profess to be conducted on European principles with a view to the convenience of English travellers, the stranger is usually made to pay smartly for clinging to his familiar customs.

From the perfect way in which things are managed in the American establishments, there is some meal in progress at every hour of the day, either breakfast, lunch, dinner, tea, or supper. Each of those meals runs on for three or four hours, a plan attained by having several rooms supplementing the great dining hall. Accordingly a man, if so minded, may begin eating at 6.30 A.M., and continue till midnight,—sleep from that hour till breakfast time again, and then—*da capo.* And this all for the 3 or 4 dollars.

Certain items are of course charged extra, as wines and liquors. All European wines are at about double home prices. There are several native wines, such as Californian champagne; but these have not yet attained the height of excellence at which they become desirable (or even happily drinkable). Bass' beer costs thirty cents or fifteenpence a pint, a price owing mainly to the excessive import duty. The beer drunk in the States is nearly always lager, a beverage brewed in the country,—but which, from a British point of view, is likely to act rather as an exhortation against thirst.

Washing is naturally another "extra." On receiving clothes for the first time from the hotel laundry, we became painfully alive to the fact that the genius of the British washerwoman does not extend to shirts; for the garments in question were brought back as glossy as ivory, and so white that, in transatlantic parlance, "chalk would have made a black mark upon them." But when the bill for this item appeared, it rather counterbalanced the pleasure we had in contemplating these monuments of the laundress's art—amounting to 2 dollars 50 cents, or 10s., for about a dozen articles! It became a serious question how to maintain at once cleanliness and economy.

In the larger American cities, the plan is much in favour of families residing permanently in hotels, each family possessing a private sitting parlour, but taking its meals at table d'hôte. This system is due to the exorbitant rents of private houses, the difficulty of getting servants to do as they are told (owing to its being a free country), and the disposition of the Americans to save themselves trouble as much as possible. American ladies prefer as a rule to visit among their friends, and spend as much money as they can in the shops, to the cares of housekeeping— a bad plan, and one which tends to undermine true domestic life. But our cousins like ease and a good (*i.e.*, a promiscuous) table better than the peaceful joys of home, and so incline to hotel life. This sort of arrangement would not suit the Briton, who delights to consider his house his castle, and who would castellate (mentally) two rooms and a kitchen, rather than live in a hotel: but the American has no ambition for a castle, his taste does not lean towards the pride of battlements; and the possession of a house not being necessary to give him his vote for Congress, he is entirely content to abide in his hotel.

These large first-class establishments can generally accommodate from six to seven hundred visitors—"guests," as Brother Jonathan puts it in a spirit of polite euphemism. And I draw this chapter to a close, by remarking that the sooner Englishmen bestir themselves and take some hints in the matter of hotel management from our friends across the water, the better.

CHAPTER III.

NEW YORK.

OUR introduction to New York was not under the most favourable circumstances, for the first day of our visit was wet and gloomy, just such a day as might have been looked for at home. The Elevated Railroad having been indicated as the best medium of transit through the city, we found our way to the Twenty-Third Street Station, an aërial structure after the "Swiss Cottage" style, approached from beneath by light iron stairways.

The Elevated Railroad is quite an "American notion," and is very convenient for hurrying citizens, though it seriously interferes with the amenity of the streets. Imagine a fine street blighted by an iron erection running along its midst on a level with the second-floor windows, cutting up the roadway with its pillared supports, and darkening all below;—then you will have a fair picture of this recent outcome of transoceanic genius. The streets through which the railroad runs may certainly be broad enough still to permit of traffic on either side of the line; nevertheless, as streets, they are spoiled.

The fare for all journeys on the Elevated Road, no matter their length, is 10 cents, or 5d.; and in paying for tickets on this initial trip we were annoyed for the first, though by no means the last time, by the smaller American coinage. Dollars, half-dollars, and quarters, are all irreproachable symbols of monetary value; but the medley of dimes, half-dimes, two and three cent pieces—silver, nickel, and copper—is very troublesome, for these lesser coins are all nearly of a size, and nickel is not unlike silver.

A train comes dashing along, is pulled up sharply at the station by the brakes, and before we are seated is off again. There is no time to bid tearful adieux to friends on the platform. The cars are light and elegant, forty or fifty feet long, with doors at each end, and passages down the middle; while the engine is a nondescript,—there are not two engines alike. Some present the appearance of ordinary carriages, their machinery being all enclosed; some are long and spidery, others short and stumpy. The favourite style of funnel is a reproduction on an enlarged scale of the rose of a watering-can, and is especially hideous. An engine and a couple of cars make up an ordinary train; and the trains succeed each other at intervals of barely five minutes. The average speed is from fifteen to twenty miles an hour, except at curves—or rather corners—which are so abrupt that the train barely crawls round. It is a pleasant mode of travelling; and you have the advantage of gaining a kaleidoscopic insight into the domestic life of New York, from the observation of the second-floor windows; the Elevated Railroad being thus considerably more lively for the passenger than the London Metropolitan. The noise of the trains does not appear to frighten horses as it might be expected to do, so that accidents seldom arise in this way: the American horse (like the American citizen), has no element of wonder in his composition—he has been accustomed to strange and fearful things from his youth upwards, and remains serenely calm in circumstances that would drive an English horse frantic.

New York is a great city, and there are many things to be seen therein: but to one set down by the Elevated Railroad in the business part of the town for the first time, there is nothing to make it strikingly apparent that he is not in a city of the old world. Commerce has a very levelling effect upon its surroundings; and people make and lose money in New York in much the same way, and in the same sort of offices and streets, as at home. The business part of New York is therefore—remarkably like the business part of any other great city!

But begin to journey outwards, and you speedily perceive a difference; advance some distance up

Broadway, with its line of warehouses and gay shops. (Broadway, be it understood, is "Broad" only in the imagination of the man who laid it out, and his mind was narrow.) The buildings are irregular, and for the most part handsome; but they are interspersed at frequent intervals with ancient and tumble-down erections, which, though no doubt interesting to the antiquarian as monuments of a past period, are most distinctly no ornament to the streets. Time, however, and an honest administration of the city revenues (if such a thing be possible), will prevail to set this right. White is a predominant colour in the buildings; and as the atmosphere is light and pure, and free from smoke, some of the streets of New York have quite a Parisian look. The roofs of the houses break forth into flags, and the "star-spangled banner" is in all its glory. Jonathan takes a singular pride in this brilliant emblem of his country, and flaunts it everywhere. Bunting manufacture must be one of the most lucrative industries of Columbia; and a comparatively brief term of years employed in this trade ought to secure to the manufacturer a very handsome independence. As a felicitous example of the harmonious disposition of colour, the flag is very pretty indeed; but repetition has a tendency to become monotonous.

The signboards of the shops have a distinctly

American character. But there are no "shops" in America; no "emporiums," no "repositories," no "bazaars:"— all are "stores." And nobody is "Hairdresser to the Queen," or " Tobacconist to the Prince of Wales:"—even the public-houses are no longer public-houses, but "saloons" and "bier-tunnels." The Briton begins to feel he is not at home. The advertisements are not home-like. "Allen's World's Hair Restorer" and "Pear's Transparent Soap" give place to "Radway's Ready Relief," "Smoke Little Joker Tobacco," and "Rising Sun Stove Polish," (the last with an illustration of much artistic atrocity). The style of these new advertisements is strange, and daringly original. Some of them take a human form,—not in the shape of placard-men with earnest adjurations borne upon their chests, not to look at their backs; but as a Red Indian in full war-paint (with clothes, however) proclaiming a patent dumb-bell; a man in knee-breeches, with doubtful calves of an inverse taper, pressing the merits of a new garter; and a Chinese (evidently of Irish extraction) setting forth the wonders of a wild beast show. Without any doubt, American invention reaches its climax in advertising.

Street vendors throng the pavement, but not to call the familiar wares. Beginning at jumping-jacks and pocket-combs, they invariably find their mission in walking-sticks and pocket-books. There are enough red leather pocket-books on New York streets to engulf our National Debt. Then you cannot go thirty yards without a solemn warning from some shop window not to blight your life's happiness by omitting to assimilate a plate of oysters, or plunge into a clam-bake. (I never dared to essay a clam-bake; but I understand it to be a preparation of shell-fish, not invariably attended with fatal consequences.) The delights of oysters hardly require to be pressed upon the Englishman; and New York is *par excellence* the place for these enticing bivalves. Oysters raw, oysters stewed, oysters fried, oyster soup—oysters in every grade of culinary embellishment greet you broadcast; and you may launch into a course of oysters without fear of materially injuring your worldly prospects, for oysters are cheap in New York.

In every eating-house window there appears a notice of "lunch." There are ordinary lunches, hot lunches, square lunches, free lunches; there is every conceivable variation of lunch. And it does not change its name as the afternoon draws out and night comes on; that is the peculiarity. In England, lunch is distinctly defined as "an insult to your breakfast, and an injury to your dinner;" but in America it remains lunch until midnight,—even till the small hours of morning. I pointed out this trifling anachronism to an American, when he turned upon me —more in sorrow than in anger, and said—

"I guess, sir, this is a free country. Isn't it now?"

"I have heard so."

"Well!" (with an indescribably delicate nasal prolongation.)

I saw that I had hurt his feelings, and regretted the occurrence.

The city of New York is admirably laid out, so that the stranger has no difficulty in finding his way. The streets running through its length are called avenues, those through its breadth simply streets; and they are distinguished by numbers, First, Second, Third, Fourth, and so on. Avenues and streets are exactly at right angles; so that the city is one of squares—*i.e.*, solid squares of building, which are known as "blocks." These blocks are of equal size, avenues and streets being respectively equi-distant. Thus there are about twenty streets to the mile up and down the city, and six avenues to the mile across; accordingly, by merely looking at the number of the street in which you happen to be, you can tell at once how far you are distant from any other street. Some of the avenues are very broad,—Third Avenue for instance, which has four lines of tramway, ample space on either side for carriages, and a line of the

Elevated Railroad on each outward extreme. A more magnificent street it would be difficult to find.

Fifth Avenue is the fashionable promenade, both for pedestrians and equipages; and at five o'clock of an afternoon the wealth and beauty of New York may be seen in full array. The New York dandy is very like the British specimen—well dressed, of average appearance,—and presumably not less beneficently endowed with intellect than any other dandy. The ladies have a certain dash and elegance in their "making up," but, as a rule, attract attention rather than admiration. They pride themselves on having the Parisian fashions earlier than any other nation, but they do not, as regards their unassisted personal charms, bear so close a survey as the fresh-looking English girl; still, there are many beautiful women amongst them.

The equipages are light and handsome; and you frequently see a negro coachman in the place of the starched and dignified English functionary. The horses are well groomed, and made to appear to their best advantage; but they are rather small, and seem often to fall away in the quarters and be lacking in power. But the place to see carriages and equestrians is Central Park, a magnificent expanse of some fifteen hundred acres, varied with drives, stretches of sward and trees, and sheets of water.

Central Park in the afternoon is the Hyde Park of New York; and there being plenty of room, the pageant moves at a lively pace, forming a pleasing contrast to the daily funeral in Hyde Park.

The Americans delight in fast-trotting horses, and low spidery vehicles seated for one, two, or four persons. That containing only one is called a "sulky;" and the idea left upon the mind by the passage of a sulky with its flying steed and solitary occupant, is that of a fellow creature resistlessly borne to an unspeakable end, entangled amid a whirling chaos of gossamer spokes. I was fortunate enough to see the park under the auspices of a friendly New Yorker and his pair of bays; but—tell it not but in a whisper—the trap, although most "correct" and sportsmanlike, was called a "buggy."

As to the sights of the city, to which tourists flock, inquiring minds are referred to any guide book: I dread inability to do them justice. There is Trinity Church, with a steeple, a corkscrew staircase (in which I irretrievably damaged my hat), and a view from the roof; there are the Post Office and the Herald Office, both massive and elegant buildings. There is the City Hall (I deeply offended a citizen by referring to it as the "Town Hall"); also Stewart's Warehouse, of white marble, and probably the largest in existence; and Tiffany's, the celebrated jeweller's, occupying the greater part of a block. There is the colossal New Suspension Bridge over the East River to Brooklyn; and there is Greenwood Cemetery in Brooklyn, four hundred and fifty acres in extent, and interesting as a cemetery,—but not enlivening. The visitor approaches it through a street bristling with monumental stones and wreaths of amaranth, as at Père la Chaise. There are two fine clubs in the city, the Union League and the Union,—with gas and every modern comfort. They are of Northern and Southern proclivities, and we were duly introduced to their privileges by the kindness of friends.

The theatres are roomy and tasteful, both in New York and throughout the States. Someone has said that, in beginning an American city, a hotel and a grand opera house are first erected, and the town gradually gathers round. Be this as it may, the theatres as houses are excellent; but the acting, although careful, generally inclines to be "stagey." It is unctuous rather than realistic, especially in the case of English plays reproduced by American artists, a feature of some surprise among a people so intensely matter-of-fact.

The means of communication between all parts of New York are admirable as regards frequency and extent. By the Elevated Railroad, and tram and omnibus systems on every street, the stranger can transport himself from place to place with pleasing facility. But there is one clamant evil,—that of overcrowding. The limit of a public conveyance is simply the number of persons it can contain by closest packing; the passengers sitting, standing, and clustering like bees upon the platform—a state of things which would be insupportable, were it not for the marvellous politeness which prevails. With the deplorable tendency to evil-speaking which obtains among a British crowd, it would be totally impossible.

The driver of a Broadway omnibus is a remarkable man. He fills the twofold capacity of driver and guard; and keeps a sharp look-out upon his passengers, receiving fares and returning change through a hole in the roof, while he threads the maze of vehicles and diffuses recrimination with happy impartiality among passing opponents.

The immediate suburbs of New York are flat and uninteresting, and under a Scotch December sky would be very dreary; but the brilliant American weather casts a glamour over the flat wastes and mean brick houses and shanties that renders them almost pleasing. The interest of the city centres in itself, and not in its surroundings: unless you direct your way seawards to Staten and Coney Islands, the summer resorts. But New Yorkers do not repair to those retreats in December; so we shall not speak of them here, but continue our journeyings, after having spent a fortnight in New York.

CHAPTER IV.

AMERICAN RAILWAYS.

BIDDING a regretful adieu to the Fifth Avenue Hotel, we left Desbrosses Street Station, Jersey City, at six o'clock one evening for Philadelphia. (A station, it must be remembered, is a "depôt" in the States.) We had heard a great deal about the marvellous luxury and convenience of American trains, and had been given to understand that a railway journey in the States was an experience of almost ecstatic bliss. "For unparalleled upholstery, the profusion of comfort, and civility of employées, our cars are without a compeer;—no other cars are a patch upon them." Such had been the words of an enthusiastic citizen, and we passively resigned ourselves to three hours of unheard-of splendour. Well;—to describe the splendour!

We emerged from the ticket office upon a shadowy expanse of dimly-lighted terminus, and made for the train. The rails were upon the same level as the platform; and the general aspect of affairs was that of recent reclamation from a wilderness. Porters were conspicuous by their absence. We encountered an American citizen who had condescended to occupy the position of guard, and addressed him :—

"Where is the smoking carriage?"

"Don't run no smoking car on this train."

"What! an American train, a three hours' journey, and no smoking car?"

"Guess you can smoke in the baggage car if you want to." And the guard turned on his heel.

The baggage car proving merely a gloomy and cavernous receptacle for trunks, we determined not to forfeit, for the sake of tobacco, the magnificence for which we were hungering; and we therefore entered an ordinary carriage. The atmosphere resembled that of a lime-kiln, dry and baking, the effect of a large stove at each end, aggravated by all the windows being closely shut. (The temperature outside was far from being very cold.) The carriage had no division from end to end, a length of some fifty feet; and low-backed seats, facing the engine, ran along each side of a long passage up the centre. These seats were each meant for two persons, and were so commodious that two full-grown men could not fail to be in closely antagonistic proximity as to knees and elbows; while to light this large apartment, the Pennsylvania Railway Company had generously provided two candles, swung in glass globes, as in the state-room of a steamer. The "dim religious light" thus produced, sufficed just to exhibit the extent of the darkness,—and was well suited to such as might desire to sleep; but 6 P.M. was rather too early for a carriageful of people to seek a common repose. Then, as if in playful irony, a newsman appeared, offering papers and magazines for sale: but naturally no one evinced an irrepressible desire to purchase. Sleep itself would have been perilous, since from the lowness of the seat-backs the sleeper's head would have depended to the rear in an uncertain and suicidal manner. Where was the wondrous luxury and refinement? Could that veracious American citizen have been romancing?

Ten minutes late, we are startled by the clangour of a most doleful bell, and the train moves off. The bell continues its solemnising tones; and looking out of the window, we find ourselves running through the middle of the streets! There is no barrier between the line and the space left for street traffic! We are electrified; we address a fellow passenger—

"Do you mean to say, sir, that in this advancing and enlightened country of yours you haven't yet enclosed your railway lines from the city streets! What have you done with all the English dollars sunk in your roads?"

"Why, we don't need any barrier; the locomotive bell rings right through the city, and people just clear off the track spontaneous. As to the dollars (with a peculiar smile),—well, I guess we've sunk a considerable number of dollars ourselves, let alone your English money; and no man knows where they are now, 'cept the directors."

" Is that the way of it? Then why don't you, as a nation, rise up and insist that your money be properly appropriated? You yourselves are the great sufferers?"

" Well, sir, we have started along doing that now; and we're cleaning the rotten boards out as lively as we can. It ain't an easy matter to strike the roots of a bad way of things all in a day. But once we do commence striking at a running abuse, we don't go to sleep till we have finished it; and we do it pretty smart too, I tell you. And we have at this time some roads in the States run under as able management as any European line. There is the New York Central; now I may say William H. Vanderbilt runs that concern with a judgment that's remarkable; the line is four track, and ballasted down as smooth as a boy's cheek; and the Central Depôt, New York City, is a sight to *ad*mire! No expense spared there, and no capital laid out that doesn't shew results."

" Don't you have a whistle on your trains? That constitutes the chief charm of a British engine."

"Why, yes, we have a whistle; but they ain't allowed to use it in the depôts or the streets. You'll hear it when we run outside the city."

We dashed through to Philadelphia at an express pace of twenty-five to thirty miles an hour, saddened at intervals by the funereal tolling of the bell. Some time before arriving, we were accosted by a gentleman, who saw that we were strangers and very politely offered his services. We always found the Americans very obliging, and ready to render us every attention; this arising partly from innate good feeling, and partly from a pride in their country, and anxiety to show it off to advantage. This gentleman—whom we afterwards found to be a member of Congress—gave us much pleasant information about the country through which we were passing, and directed us to the Continental Hotel, Philadelphia, where he also took up his quarters. By his advice we entrusted our portmanteaus to an express-man, or parcel delivery official, and proceeded to the hotel by tram-car; a plan which Americans themselves generally follow, to save the enormous cab fares. And before parting, he was so courteous as to present us with his card, saying that he would be glad to see us at his home in a Western city, should we incline thither.

And now to say a little about the American railway system—gathered of course from subsequent experience in our journeyings.

America is a Republic, and her railways are Republican. The cars are all of one class, and open from end to end. Jack is as good as his master; and this principle is supposed to constitute a free country. But in whatever degree the proposition with regard to Jack may be applicable to a future existence, the fact remains—that in this world Jack is not as good as his master. If he were as good, he would not long remain Jack. The Americans have sufficient sense to admit this to themselves, but are pleased to keep up the pretence of ignoring it. There are distinctions of rank and class in the States, as clearly, if not as haughtily defined as in any other country; therefore the cloak of affectation should be thrown off, and such reforms made as only await the casting of the cloak. True liberty consists in every man being free to rise;—certainly not in all men being considered on an equality while as yet they occupy widely different positions in the social scale.

The disadvantage of having no nominally separate classes on American trains, is met by there being a Pullman or Wagner car on nearly every train, for the use of which travellers pay an extra sum. People might call it a first class; but don't like to do so, in case Jack's *amour propre* should be hurt. (This shows rare delicacy of feeling.) The Pullman car has long been famous; and as it has now been introduced into this country, people may judge of its qualities for themselves. Our conclusion with regard to it was, that however splendid in its fittings, it could not compete with the English carriage in solid comfort. It seemed to bear the same relation to an English first class carriage, as a modern drawing-room does to a cosy parlour or smoking-room: in the drawing-room there are elegance and style, with impossible chairs, aërial sofas, tidies, and the like feminine inventions; in the parlour there are great roomy chairs, with (not improbably) a place whereon to raise your feet. Now we do not care to travel in a drawing-room; we do not want splendour, only ease. And the English carriage, with its padded sides and deep cushions and arm rests, appears to give more real ease than the Pullman.

There are three sorts of Pullman cars,—drawing-room cars, sleeping-cars, and dining cars. On a short journey, you find only the first named; but on a trip of twenty-four hours or more, you have the others in addition.

The sleeping car appears by day as a "parlour-car," with velvet covered benches; but as night draws on, the gilded roof-panels are opened up, blankets and snowy linen taken out, and two tiers of regular berths made up on each side. The berths are beautifully neat and clean; and the apartment is curtained off into sections. The immediate agent of this metamorphosis is the coloured porter in attendance on each car. You retire within your berth, and corkscrew yourself into a posture nearly indescribable and wholly agonising (it may be imperfectly portrayed by saying that you tie your body in a knot); then you wrestle with your clothes till you have attained the garb of night, while your head bumps playfully against the berth above. It becomes the nicest of problems how to preserve at once an unbroken skull and strict propriety. In these terrible struggles an untrousered leg may sometimes be seen flourishing beyond the curtain; when the black porter is down upon the offender like a hawk, with a stern injunction to "retire within himself" and maintain the *morale* of the car.

Once ensconced in your berth, you have a capital sleep; the only drawback being the close atmosphere. In the morning you undergo reinsertion into your garments in the same circumscribed way, and take your turn with the other passengers in a nice lavatory at the end of the car; then the black porter assaults you vigorously with a straw clothesbrush, and your toilet is complete. These conveniences for lengthened travel are very pleasant when you have become used to them.

The dining car is just the dining room of a hotel on a reduced and perambulating system, where all meals are provided at reasonable charges; obviating the need for a sudden and severe combat with the comestibles at a wayside refreshment-room.

A Pullman car is said to cost about £4000, and an ordinary American car £1400.

One advantage, our cousins tell us, of their car, is that you can move about and talk to the other occupants. But that is just what we least wish to do. We are not a talkative people to strangers. The Briton is self-contained; the American is gregarious. The American is not happy alone, he must ease his tongue; and if he cannot find a friend within reach, he fixes upon the first likely-looking stranger. The flow of his ideas is irresistible, and must find an outlet.

Another superiority of the long divisionless cars, we were constantly informed, lay in their having a door on to the platform at either end, which could be opened at will. At home, it was alleged, we were always locked in. I tried to point out that we were not always locked in, but only when safety demanded it, to prevent passengers from getting out on the wrong side in the way of passing trains; but no, no explanation could be received;—we were sometimes locked in, and that was enough. To the American mind this was an enormity. It seemed to strike at the very roots of personal freedom. They asked, "What would you do in case of an accident?" I said, "Sit still and hold on,—what would you?" They were never quite certain; but seemed to think it would be more in accordance with the liberty of the citizen to throw themselves out headlong on the rails on their individual responsibility. I said that rather than risk so profound an uncertainty, I thought I would prefer to await "telescoping;" but they shook their heads wisely, and looked disapproval.*

A very free and easy style prevails on the American train. People stand outside on the platforms, walk from one carriage to another while the train is in motion, take an occasional turn into the baggage car, and consult their individual inclinations in every way. They do not settle down for the journey as an Englishman does. On a hot day in summer they throw open all the windows, to give free ingress to fresh air—and dust; and the occupants of the smoking car (there generally is one, though we were unlucky in our first experience) occasionally sit with their feet tilted outside the window, to woo the grateful breeze about their trouser legs. A passing

* The *Chicago Times*, a leading American newspaper, in describing the recent lamentable Tay Bridge accident, refers to the passengers in the ill-fated train as having been "locked in by barbarous British conservatism."

train with a flitting vision of boot-soles disposed in this graceful way is an interesting sight.

The guard and brakesman are important functionaries, and novel in their respective styles. The brakesman is quite the lesser luminary of the two. The brakes are not worked from the engine and goods-van simply, but on each separate car; and each car has its proper brakesman, for the guard is far exalted above such office. The brakesman sits at the end of his car, among the passengers, running out to the platform to work his wheel as occasion demands; thus the brake cannot be applied so instantaneously as at home. A spring brake is that most in use, which is wound up in readiness, and falls whenever the spring is released. On goods trains the brakes are worked by wheels on the roofs of the waggons; and the men may be seen running along the roofs like so many monkeys—bitter and slippery work in winter time.

The guard is a magnate of much presence. He does not answer to "guard;" but must be invoked as "conductor," and even then deferentially. He is resplendent in uniform and buttons, has a peculiarly ugly cap, and weighs between fifteen and twenty stone. I hardly saw a railway conductor in the States whose girth could have been less than fifty inches. Railway shareholders are lean; but directors and conductors are always fat,—especially the latter. The conductor carries a supply of tickets, which he dispenses during the journey to such passengers as have not secured them at the station, and receives their fares. He is far above his English brother,—he would wither with a glance the unhappy man who ventured to offer him a "tip;"—such a miserable proceeding would be derogatory to him. In bygone days, he was wont to find it more in keeping with his dignity to appropriate so much of the railway's moneys passing through his hands, as he might consider a due recompense for his services: but this practice, I am happy to think, is now a thing of the past, and the American conductor may claim with his fellow men a fair character for honesty. A capital story is told of one of these conductors of the olden time. This man occupied his place for some years on a moderate salary, and was known to have no private means; but a marked increase became continually apparent in his worldly prosperity, till he was finally seen the owner of a neat villa, no mean acreage, and cattle to match. Then the Board of management, deeming his conduct to have been unfeelingly glaring, and hoping to air their own rectitude by his dismissal, called him before them one day in solemn meeting, and spoke gently as follows:—

"Conductor O'Brien, we have been unwillingly compelled to notice that your circumstances have undergone a material change of late. You have built a house and bought land, and appear before your neighbours in a sphere which your salary fails to warrant. Unpleasant comments are being made. There is, of course, but one inference to which we are, however reluctantly, led; and being willing to avoid unpleasant exposure, we have agreed to dismiss you without more question. You have nothing to say?"

Quoth the conductor blandly:—

"Gentlemen, I appreciate your feelings and the kindly tone in which they are uttered, and admit that I may have been injudicious. But I shall make one remark. Gentlemen, you have remarked upon my house, and my land, and my cattle, and mean to dismiss me. Well, I reckon you must get another man in my place. And I just want to remind you, that while I have now got these things, and am satisfied, the other man will come without them, *and will have to get them!*"

And the Board did not ponder long, but retained him.

There is one constant pest on American trains which cannot be passed over—namely, the book-agent. This individual is called a book-agent, but is really a common nuisance; and there is hardly any commodity under the sun that he is not agent for. He has a great receptacle in one of the cars, something between a plate-chest and a mediæval coffin, out of which he brings one evil thing after another, till you can liken him to none but Herr Dobler or the Wizard of the North. He appears first, probably, with an armful of books; and shrewdly judging from the appearance of his victim whether the latter's taste be solid, sensational, or theological, he selects a corresponding publication, and calmly places it upon the victim's knee. Returning in five minutes, he reclaims the book, and vanishes. In twenty minutes more he is back again, armed this time with a basket of oranges and sweetmeats,—pestering everyone to buy. This sort of thing goes on through the entire journey. The resources of that man are endless; his "reserved power," as Professor Matthews would say, is terrific. He is a fiend in human shape, utterly without feeling. His delight seems almost to lie more in tormenting than in effecting sales. With the constantly recurring visits of this demon, sleep is of course impossible: and the moral effect alone of such an infliction upon the passengers, in the development of contumely, is incalculable. Surely the Americans must be alive to this plague; I only marvel that they suffer it to go on.

The luggage system on American trains is perfect. The traveller, on buying his ticket, gives up his belongings to the baggage man, and receives for each article a brass check, the counterpart of which is affixed to the article. Then he may travel on for days and nights, without ever troubling himself to look after his luggage; and, on delivering up his checks at the journey's end, there are the "traps" safe and sound. This check system makes the railway directly responsible, and saves all annoyance. Further, when alighting from the train, the passenger may hand over his checks to the omnibus man or the parcel delivery agent (who come on to the train), and so have his luggage taken directly up to the hotel. Why we, in Britain, have not yet adopted so obvious an improvement on our own confused system, is a question to be answered by those in charge of our passenger arrangements.

The American locomotive is a curious structure, very different from our massive tight-built engine. It is cumbrous and unwieldy, with a large glass-house for the driver, and an enormous bell-mouthed chimney. The latter is made wide to ensure the perfect combustion of the fuel, which is chiefly wood, and to prevent sparks from doing damage to the dry country round; a wire netting, indeed, is stretched across the top, to keep the larger particles of burning fuel from escaping. The boiler is long and low, with shining brass bands; and there is an appearance of flimsiness and tinsel about the whole locomotive. In front there is the great wooden cowcatcher,—which is not unnecessary, as the line has in many places no continuous barrier between it and the adjoining fields, to check the wandering propensities of stray cattle. The entire engine is suggestive rather of an ironmonger's shop than an engine yard; and you cannot associate with so clumsy a fabric the idea of speed; yet these locomotives are said to be capable of attaining a rate nearly as high as our own.

Most American trains run slowly—some very slowly; the average speed being about twenty-five miles an hour. (There is even a line in a back district, I am told, where progress is so slow that the cowcatcher is shifted and put on behind!) But the reason of this want of pace does not seem far to seek: the United States railways cover a vast extent of territory; and such capital as the nation can yet afford is inadequate to the perfect levelling and finishing of these lengthened tracks; while an increase of speed means also a proportionate increase in the wear and tear of rolling stock by friction. And as most of the American railways are financially in straitened circumstances, an improvement in speed cannot be early looked for.

Railway fares are cheap in the States, a very gratifying feature; three cents a mile being the maximum charge for ordinary travelling.

The mode of constructing a new railway through a district not taken up by settlers is somewhat remarkable. The company for the projected line having satisfied Government that it will be a public benefit, and having obtained permission to proceed with their operations, the Government gives them large grants of land adjoining the track, which they dispose of to settlers, and thus realise so much against cost. The laying down of the line is effected with a rapidity that would strike a British contractor dumb. The country is probably prairie or flat land; in which case farmers move on in front with their ploughs and turn up the soil, while the workmen follow quickly behind, levelling, laying down the rails, and ballasting as they find material. There is often a great scarcity of stone ballast; and in order to strengthen the track as much as possible, the sleepers are placed very close together—only some eighteen inches apart. The workmen live in cars, which are pushed onwards as the line progresses; and they are frequently divided into shifts, working day and night. A mile of roadmaking in the day has been known to be accomplished in this peculiar (though it can hardly be called *permanent*) way.

As years go on and the country yields an increasing traffic, the line is slowly improved; but for a long time it remains very rough and uneven.

And now, our first railway journey having brought us to the Continental Hotel, Philadelphia, we pass on to the wonders of the Quaker City.

CHAPTER V.

THE QUAKER CITY.

THE Continental Hotel, Philadelphia, proved to be one of the most perfect of the great American hotels. There was an air of homely comfort blended with its magnificence, which made our sojourn very pleasant; and Mr Kingsley, the proprietor, took a kindly interest, not only in our welfare within doors, but in our rambles through the city, and gave us his best aid in indicating what was to be seen.

The hotel waiters were all black men; and from Philadelphia south and westward we always had the negro servitor. In majesty of bearing the coloured waiter comes short of his white brother; but he more than makes up for it in expression. The component parts of a black waiter are a white waistcoat, a large collar, two rows of glistening teeth, and a smile—scarcely a smile either—something between a broad laugh and a yawn. The black waiter is always smiling; more, I think, from inborn good nature than from any acute perception of the ridiculous. I am hardly able to estimate with certainty the size of his mouth when at rest, having always seen it wreathed in a grin; and I should therefore be inclined to describe it as a latitudinal cavity, bounded by the ears. These negroes are all obliging to a degree, and seem to find their greatest happiness in ejaculating " Yis sa!" and rushing to execute an order. As a rule they are excellent waiters; but you occasionally meet with one of an amusing type, who either forgets what is ordered, and brings a great array of dishes on chance; or, if he does bring what he is told, he includes two or three extra dishes out of the fulness of his heart. Now, there are two qualifications equally needful for a good waiter,—first, to know what you want,—and second, to know what you do not want. In the latter the negro is sometimes deficient; but he is always good tempered; and the more trouble you give him, the prouder he appears.

The first day we spent in Philadelphia was a Sunday; and we were surprised to find a pantomime being performed in a theatre close beside the hotel. And this in the very heart of the Quaker City, with its reputed jealousy for Sunday observance and religious propriety! America is a strange mixture.*

Churches in America show a great advance on the like edifices at home, in that the seats are constructed with a view to comfort, and with a proper consideration of the lines of the human frame. There

* This violation, however, has since been summarily dealt with.

is no *peine forte et dure*, as in an old-fashioned Scotch kirk, where the seats are engines of penance and self-mortification: the American does not think of sitting in a series of right angles; he has an inviting curve at his back; and as decency forbids his elevating his feet to the level of his head during service, he at least provides that there be ample room to stretch his legs. A small matter this, it may be said;—and yet hardly so small,—for a straight-backed pew has often militated wofully against an excellent doctrine.

It was in Philadelphia, towards the end of December, that we experienced the first hard frost of the year. The thermometer indicated twelve degrees below freezing point; and the air was sharp and clear, with none of the dampness which attends an English frost, and points to a speedy thaw. There was no humidity, but a wonderful feeling of exhilaration; so that, although cold, it was splendid weather for sight-seeing.

Fairmount Park and the Centennial Exhibition Buildings are perhaps the most interesting sights to a stranger. The former is to Philadelphia what Central Park is to New York; and it is an immense place, 3200 acres in extent,—more like an embryo State than a civic park. The boundaries do not, however, seem to be quite defined as yet; and there appears to be a good deal of the " howling wilderness" about its outer confines. But the side nearest the city is highly civilized, with capital drives and footpaths, and trimly-cut borders; and here the Philadelphians turn out to drive in the afternoon. Even in winter time they can enjoy their park until nearly six P.M.,—so much difference is there between the length of their winter day and our own.

The observant stranger will remark that almost every citizen of the Republic appears to possess, or have some interest in, a horse. Horses are cheap, more especially in the West; for £20 a creditable animal can be procured, and a tolerable imitation of one for half the money. And here two curious phases of national character would present themselves for contrast. The British shop-boy, in the attempt to assimilate his appearance with that of a stable-helper, saves his meagre earnings to purchase a dust overcoat of a sporting cut, and a pair of trousers so attenuated as to assure the beholder that he put his boots on last; the American lad, on the other hand, is content to appear as Nature (and his employer) designed him, but would almost seem to invest his spare capital in the part-ownership of a quadruped.

The buildings in which the Centennial Exhibition of 1877 was held adjoin the park. Part has been taken down; but a large structure still remains, which is used as a permanent exhibition. The Philadelphia

Exhibition possessed this advantage over European rivals,—that it had no lack of space. There is plenty of room in America for such displays. (I do not understand, however, that the moral character of the hotel proprietors and lodging-house keepers, during the Exhibition, was any higher than that of their European brethren in similar circumstances.)

We visited also the Baldwin Locomotive Works, probably the most extensive of their kind in the country; and afterwards we had a look at the Russian privateers, then in course of being fitted out in Cramp's Yard, for use against our mercantile marine. (How Brother Jonathan would have reconciled this little transaction with his " Alabama Claims," in the event of an Anglo-Russian war, is barely apparent; but with Jonathan business is business, and he trusts to his "'cuteness" to keep him clear of trouble.)

Philadelphia is to the non-commercial traveller the most uninteresting city in the States. It is built on a dead flat, like most American cities, and planned with wearisome mathematical exactitude. In New York we occasionally found the street to take a bend ; in Philadelphia never. Interminable, too, are these Philadelphia streets—many of them laid out for miles and miles without a break. Distances are great, and outside the heart of the city the houses are rather scattered.

We were seated in the hotel after a day's monotonous rambling, beside a close shaven "wide-awake" looking gentleman, who occupied himself for some time in a meditative survey of our appearance. At last, having evidently gathered from his scrutiny sufficient data on which to base a conversation, he removed a very black cigar from his mouth, and addressed us :—

" From Europe, gentlemen ? "

" Yes. Have we the stamp of recent arrival ? "

" Well, I can see you weren't raised right here ; it don't take the gift of prophecy to tell that. And how do you like the country? What do you think of our city ? "

"The country is pretty good as you get used to it ; but I can't say we are particularly struck with Philadelphia."

" Not *ad*mire Philadelphia! (with emotion). Now, I consider Philadelphia's a city can't be beat in the Union. Why, what do you find to complain of ? "

" The place is terribly spread out for its size. It is quite a journey from one part to another."

" Too much spread out! I guess when we have nine hundred thousand inhabitants in a place, we like to let them breathe. We don't want them confined and crowded up. We lay out our cities on approved sanit*airy* principles ; and Philadelphia is top city of the list in that particular. And when you want to move around, you have the tram-cars: can't you ride?"

"We tried that once or twice, and got shaken to bits on your cobble-stones. I don't like a tramway line laid over boulders. It may be good after dinner as a digestive, but it's not pleasant."

(Reflectively) "Well now, that may be so; I never thought of that. But our streets and blocks—you find them elegant and regular, don't you?"

"My dear sir, your streets are straight enough in all conscience, but they're saddening. If a man were to see his whole future life stretching clear before him to its end, he would most likely sit down and despair of ever getting on; now, it's pretty much the same with a Philadelphia street. You look cheerlessly along a rigid line—down an endless vista of houses and signboards—and feel that somewhere on the horizon, where the last tramway car meets the sky, you will find the point you wish to go to. And the prospect isn't inspiring."

"Now, that's what I call a real old world notion. It's clearly silly. It ain't utilitarian. If I want to go to a place, I strike a bee line for it. I mean to get there, and I don't go fooling around corners. But your view of the matter is essentially British, sir. There's no doubt of that. I've been in England myself, and I know what it is. If I'm in one of your large cities, and I ask my way anywhere, your Englishman puts his finger to his head and thinks a spell; then he says:—' Queen Street? Yes. Yes, of course. Take the third turning to the left, then go on and turn to the right, and you'll come to a square; then take the street leading out of the square on the side next to this, and go on for a bit; then turn a corner to the right, and strike through a lane, and you're there.' Well, I do as I'm told, and I go through the square, and round the corner, and down the lane:—and then I'm *not* there. And then I get mad, and take a cab. Now, sir, life's too short for that kind of folly. A business man has no time for it."

"Well, I'm afraid we can't uphold our case against such a practical demonstration. There's no question that Philadelphia is a great city; and as a commercial centre you may fairly be proud of it. Cloth manufacture is your staple industry, is it not?"

"Chiefly, I should say. We had the shipbuilding of the States before the war; but that's played out for the present. Between import duties on materials, and high wages, our shipbuilding is at a standstill."

"I suppose if protection were abolished, the trade would spring up again fast?"

"Right away. We showed the world, in the days of wooden ships, that we could turn out as fine craft as any other nation; and I guess we won't be behind with iron vessels when we can start again. It won't be long either. Twenty years ago we were forced to protection; but the country is finding it don't need it any longer now, and the days of a purely revenue tariff, like that of Britain, will soon come."

"The sooner the better, I should say, for us as well as you."

"Why, sir, it's a crying evil, as things stand; we are prevented not only from building ships, but even from owning foreign-built vessels. At least, we can't have foreign ships registered in the States. Now, if these restrictions were removed, we would compete with you in the carrying trade of the world; at present we haven't even a carrying trade of our own! Our goods are carried mainly under foreign flags. In Philadelphia here, we have the only American steam passenger line to Europe that runs from the Northern States. No, sir,—don't go to suppose that this state of things will last long!"

"Your large American cities seem to be built with splendid facilities for water conveyance, being situated either on the seaboard or by your great rivers or lakes."

"That's so: we take care of that. That's the advantage of being a new country; we locate a new city right in the most advantageous spot for trade.

We look ahead and see the trade in prospect; then we start along and build the city to suit. In Europe it's mostly different. Some thieving chap in the middle ages would plant a castle on a mountain, to be safe from his enemies, or to have a handsome view; then a crew of miserable peasants, that depended upon him, and lived in terror of their necks, gathered around. Then as time went on, and the country got settled, more people would come around and build houses, and make a city of the place;—with likely a grand statue of the old rogue in the middle of it, and an inscription stating him to have been the Benefactor of the Locality and the Father of Commercial Enterprise. And there they would fix themselves down to live and trade, although there mightn't be a single feature about the spot to make it really suitable for commerce. That's the old-fashioned European plan, you'll observe. Now I guess we've risen a bit on that."

"Well, there's no doubt that you seem to pitch your cities just where they will be of most use to you. Although I don't entirely concur in your sweeping summary of European towns. But we won't go into such matters of detail. Can you tell me, now, how property stands in Philadelphia—are house rents as high here as in New York?"

"No; we are considerably below New York figures

here. Besides, real estate has shrunk greatly of late. A three-floor house and basement, such as a merchant would like to live in, will run about 10,000 dollars cost, or some 700 dollars rental."

We rarely found Americans otherwise than willing to give information, and ready to talk on any subject that might come up. In fact, the confidence which they volunteered on their own private affairs, and the freedom with which they condemned the faults of their own legislature, as well as of ours, were often surprising.

A somewhat melancholy national characteristic forced itself on our notice in Philadelphia, and was borne out by subsequent experience—the tendency of the male American to black clothes. In New York this was apparent; but as New York is the centre of American fashion—and even American fashion is European—it was not so marked in that city. But in Philadelphia it was universal, and most depressing to the stranger. It is a city of long-tailed black coats, sepulchral trousers, and sombre wide-awake hats. Can this costume have been born of the Pilgrim Fathers?

CHAPTER VI.

"THE CITY OF MAGNIFICENT DISTANCES."

BIDDING adieu to the Quaker City, we turned our course towards Washington, an afternoon's journey. Washington, as the headquarters of the American legislature, is not situated in any one State, lest invidious comparisons should arise; but possesses a little territory of its own, some few miles square, named the " District of Columbia," after the whole country. And the centre of American politics thus generally appears as " Washington, D. C.," to distinguish it from the multifarious Washingtons scattered through the breadth of the land.

The railway passed along the side of the Delaware for some distance, and across the Susquehanna farther on. Those streams were spanned chiefly by rough wooden trestle-bridges; and the train just crept over, apparently from a sense of insecurity. The country on either side of the line was much like lowland Scotland; cultivated fields alternating with low hills and pine woods; while most of the trees were old friends—beech, ash, oak, and fir. At times we crossed a stretch of moorland (but without the heather), and again ran through a swamp. Though by no means "Far West," the country, especially in its bleak December aspect, seemed rather primitive, with frequent signs of very recent clearing from its native wood. There were no stone walls, the fields and "lots" being divided by fences of very patriarchal simplicity. All the farm-houses and cottages were of wood, generally painted white.

We bowled along at an unusually fair speed, sometimes approaching to forty miles an hour, passed through Baltimore, an important seaport and manufacturing city, and reached Washington at sundown. The last rays of the sun were striking on the massive dome of the great marble Capitol; and we were fairly fascinated. So grand a sight was it, that all Washington seemed naturally to merge in the Capitol—we saw nothing else. It was a rare thing for either of us to fall into raptures about architectural magnificence; we were not inclined to draw romance from a column, or inspiration from a gurgoyle :—but this great white American Capitol was truly majestic.

Washington is a unique city. It has 140,000 inhabitants, and yet is wholly uncommercial. The life-blood and sole vital principle of the place is politics; *i.e.*, in the wide sense, as embracing not only the Legislative Assemblies, but also the various departmental functions of Government, such as the

Treasury, the Post Office, the Patent Office, and even the Arsenal and Navy Yard. Many of the population are employées in these departments; three thousand persons are employed in the Treasury alone.

In no American city so much as in Washington do the magnificent and the mean stand in such striking juxtaposition. Close beside splendid Government Buildings cower the paltriest of houses and most miserable of shanties. Washington has been well named the "City of magnificent distances." Like a boy's clothes, it has been laid out for its growth. The streets and avenues are very fine, but many of them have only a few wooden houses dotting their length at wide intervals. If the city can be filled up according to the present ambitious plan, it has a future of splendour before it, and will yet vie with any European capital; but to this end money and time are wanted,—and it is probable that the second will arrive sooner than the first.

The main points of interest in Washington are the Capitol, the White House, the Treasury, the Secretary of State's Department, the Patent Office, the Navy Yard, and the Arsenal,—a pretty fair list. The great attraction centres in the Capitol. This remarkable building is all of white marble, to which, equally with its size and perfect architecture, it owes its magnificence. Its area is vast; and the grandeur of its architecture lies in its complete simplicity. A frequent tendency of the American architect is to gingerbread and ornament, and thus many an otherwise fine building is spoiled; but the Capitol has escaped this, and stands by itself, at once a model and a marvel. It consists of two wings, with a centre compartment surmounted by a dome. One of these wings is given up to the Senate, the other to the Assembly of Representatives; those two bodies bearing respectively a certain resemblance to our own Houses of Lords and Commons. The Representatives are elected every second year by the nation, every male over twenty years of age voting; the Senators for six years, by the several State Legislatures. Both Senators and Representatives have an annual salary of 5000 dollars, or £1000.

Our visit unluckily falling at Christmas-time, the Houses were not in session; the wise men of America having all gone home to consume their turkey in the bosom of their families. But we had free access to the Capitol; and that, be it remarked, without having to press the palm of an attendant policeman, as in our own august Halls of Parliament. There was no Cerberus at the door—hardly even an official to be seen anywhere; all and sundry were allowed to roam over the place as they listed. (And there were some very "shady" specimens of the American citizen visible.) The interior of the Houses was not so remarkable as the exterior might lead one to expect; for, while decidedly handsome, it was in no way extraordinary. A startlingly free and easy style prevailed throughout,—smoking went on everywhere, and expectoration was at its height. Spittoons adorned every corner; yet more—each individual Senator's and Representative's chair was furnished with a spittoon. Notices certainly were posted up, requesting persons to prefer these utensils to the carpets and the marble floor; but the whole fact of such a custom was strange and horrible. This, and suchlike freedoms are the *exaggerated* "notions" of a "free country." What a sensation would be caused if any member or visitor attempted to smoke a cigar in Westminster!—It would be worse even than Irish obstruction!

The Legislative (and Expectorative) Assemblies have every convenience within their Capitol. Bodily nourishment and personal cleanliness are provided for, by a large restaurant devoted to divers meats and strange drinks, and a *suite* of lavatories and hot baths. Nor are the wants of the mind forgotten, witness an extensive library, containing 320,000 volumes. Free use of this library is granted to the public. A catalogue is now being compiled, which will itself contain 12,000 pages!

"THE CITY OF MAGNIFICENT DISTANCES."

We climbed the dome, a height of two hundred feet, by an ascent of three hundred steps, and had a far-spreading view around; but the prospect could not justly be called beautiful, owing to the extreme flatness of the country. On the top of the dome is a bronze statue of Liberty, eighteen feet high without its pedestal, which reflects the beams of the sun so as to appear from a distance like a dazzling spot of fire. (Statues of Liberty in America are as common as nuts in October.) At the summit of the cupola there was a stand on which photographs and the like were exposed for sale. Stalls for photographs, sweetmeats, cooling syrups, *et hoc genus omne*, pervaded the whole building,—a trifling circumstance in itself, nevertheless important as pointing to the fact that America is essentially a commercial country. Every facility is given to the huckster and costermonger for the conduct of his business; and he shows by his extreme enterprise that he is not unworthy of the encouragement.

The White House is the residence of the President. Like the Capitol, it is of white marble: it is long and rather low, with massive columns at the doorway; and the façade is pleasing. It looks almost homely, yet withal it is dignified. There are no surrounding grounds to speak of; and an unpretentious carriage drive through open gates leads up to the portico on either side. Strangers are not only free to call upon the President, but their doing so is esteemed a mark of courtesy; accordingly we approached the awful portal one morning, intent on presentation. Our purpose of calling had been hasty; so we were clad in ordinary travelling tweeds, and felt rather conscious of the fact. There was no sentry on guard at the door, no liveried official of any kind—only a plain man in every-day dress, who showed us into a waiting-room. Davis said to him, in a deprecatory tone—

"I'm afraid we are scarcely correct enough in costume to meet the President."

"All right sir, all right; this isn't a reception day, and the President will be glad to see you in any dress. There's a party just paying their respects now; but if you'll give me your cards, I'll take you right up whenever they have done."

"Does the President see every one who comes to call?"

"Any person who don't come seeking for office. We have a lot of them; but we get to know that kind pretty well, and keep them out. They have got to see the President elsewhere, if they want to apply to him. But we are always pleased to see strangers."

At this juncture an American citizen came in, and announced his intention of interviewing the great man. This gentleman's appearance completely relieved us of all doubts as to the propriety of our own; for the fact that he possessed clothes was all that he could boast. He was an agriculturist from the far west, and seemed to have been recently dug up from his native soil,—and to have suffered considerably in the process. His boots were capacious and muddy, the light of day peeped through a fissure in his coat-tails, and his hat,—well, it had once been a hat. But his eye flashed with the "Eagle Glance of Freedom," as he proceeded to "fix" a very dirty collar before the gilt mirror; and he "guessed he would step right in" whenever the President was disengaged. He gave his name as "William B. Hoskin, from Whitesville, Nebraska."

The President sat in his private room, with his secretary beside him; and we were ushered in in rear of this child of liberty, to witness the following interview :—

President Hayes: "Good morning, Mr Hoskin!" (And the pair shook hands warmly). "Just arrived in Washington?"

"Came in by this morning's train, President. Goin' east to Baltimore, and thought I'd jest step around on the way."

"And how are things in Whitesville? Are you farming out there?"

"Doin' the best I can with a hundred-acre lot. Corn didn't come on this year as speedy as usual; but if we git a good winter and an airly spring, I calculate we'll come boomin' up next season."

"Well, sir, I'm glad to have met you. *Good* morning." (Another handshake, and *exit* citizen with an easy bearing).

Then turning to us, with another digital vibration,—

"How do you do, gentlemen? From Scotland, I see."

"Yes, sir."

"Aha! I've a warm corner in my heart for Scotland. You have been having bad times there, though, these last months."

"Very bad indeed."

"Business, I suppose, at its very worst. Are you making a tour of the States?"

"We are just beginning to do so."

"Well, gentlemen, I hope you will find it pleasant, and carry back agreeable recollections of America. And now, I must bid you good morning, as I have a good deal to do." (More handshaking, a general kotoo, and *eximus*, both sides smiling).

President Hayes is a pleasant elderly man, with an easy and courteous address; but he must find it no small infliction to receive such a promiscuous horde of callers, and to hold himself politely at the disposal of every free and independent citizen in a flannel shirt and a battered hat, who chooses to invade him. But his term of office lasts only four years; and he doubtless knew what was before him when he "ran" for the Presidency.

The total absence of form and ceremony in the presence of the highest dignitary of the United States, a country with a population something like a fifth greater than that of Great Britain and Ireland, is to the stranger very remarkable, and, at first, not altogether pleasing. But America has ways of her own, in which she began, and to which she will hold: and in these particulars she is so entirely different from European nations, that it is quite impossible to draw parallels. In order to understand American ways, and the suitability with which they work, one must personally know the American people. Many American methods would never do in the Old World; but they certainly succeed in the New,—and even appear to be the best attainable there, despite attendant evils. America is the natural paradise of immigration—for all nationalities, from all quarters of the globe; and being well aware that in this ever-flowing tide lies the spirit of her strength, she gives it every encouragement. These constant new arrivals, leaving their homes from all manner of causes,—political, social, or pecuniary,—would not seek a country where the government was hereditary, and where ideas ran in the fixed groove inevitable to a hereditary government. They each bring with them ideas of their own, believing that these ideas will find play in America: some, indeed, they are forced to surrender; but others they retain, and the last are amalgamated with the nation's system, just as their holders fuse into the national whole. (So many persons have sought the New World from political troubles in the land of their birth, that America has been humorously defined as "The safety-valve of European Monarchy!")

America, as she stands, seems to have grasped in its full broad sense the idea of liberty, *without* the evils of "equality" and "fraternity" which attend similar attempts on this side of the ocean. The secret of this is,—that America *is simply going on as she began:* she started as a nation with certain ideas of national freedom, and has been able in a natural and unchallenged way to preserve these. Unfortunately, she uses a good deal of bombast in proclaiming her views to the world, and thus damages to many onlookers the appearance of a principle which is really being successfully put in practice. But exaggeration and "tall talk" will die out as the nation grows older; and so also will many minor evils disappear; for this certainly can be said of America,—that when she does recognise a thing to be an evil, she sets herself resolutely—and speedily—to uproot it. The spirit, then, of the American's love of his form of government is this: he admires and respects all good men set over him in power—the more because he as an individual has had his share in placing them there; but, though himself only a rough western settler, he has the distinct feeling that he too, by ability and persevering industry, may rise to a like honourable position. The prairie herd-boy sees in himself a future president, and so whistles Yankee Doodle with increased vivacity, and tends his cattle with the greater care. Therefore, America and England must be looked at separately, each in its peculiar way, and each on its own merits.

The Treasury, the Secretary of State's Department, and the Patent Office are fine buildings,—notably the second. In the Treasury we saw the greenbacks, or American paper money, in process of being struck; a large number of young women being employed in connection with this. An American greenback is long and narrow, and for some time does not impress the Briton with the same feeling of self-respect as the possession of a five-pound Bank of England note.

In the Patent Office is kept a model of every

patent taken out in the States: and the collection is naturally a very interesting one. A strong incentive to inventive genius is offered in America by the cheapness and ease of obtaining a patent, the cost being only about £10. Americans were at the outset forced to invention, by the fact of their country's having then too few hands to do its work, so that a greater need of machinery asserted itself. But while the former imperative necessity is now past, owing to the vastly-increased population, invention still goes briskly on; the reason being, not that the American is cleverer than the Englishman, but that he can more easily bring forward his idea. In both countries the working mechanic is the principal inventor, because from daily practical familiarity with his calling, and its existing machinery, he is naturally the first to see possible improvements. In England the working-man can seldom afford the cost of bringing out a patent, so his idea too often dies with himself; but in the States it is otherwise, and there the genius of the artisan has every encouragement. It has been urged that cheapness of patenting would flood the land with useless inventions; but even this could do no harm. Many a useful idea would come to light that at present is crushed and confined within a single breast; and as for the worthless, they would simply die a natural death, without any one being a whit the worse.

The Navy Yard, like the other national institutions, is open to all visitors: and a very waste and desolate place did it look on our visit;—though there are probably more signs of life about it in summer. The Potomac was covered with ice, and all the vessels were laid up for the winter. Five or six monitors lay at the wharf, one of which, the "Passaig," we boarded, and were met by as surly a tar as ocean ever produced;—politeness, in truth, to such a man, was a pure waste of good material. But we extracted a good deal of information from the master of a government tow-boat, who was as obliging as the old salt was offensive.

The monitors are wicked-looking little boats, drawing twelve or thirteen feet, with only two feet of freeboard. Each one is armed with a couple of nine-ton guns, mounted in a revolving turret. They are intended solely for coast defence, and are bad sea-boats. They can steam only nine knots an hour,—a fact which rather surprised us, as one of the essential requisites of such craft is speed. The monitor is designed for use against the large ironclad; and for this purpose she should be able to move with great rapidity, and be easily turned and handled, so as to play round the big ship, which, from her unwieldiness, cannot so readily change position.

The United States' Navy possesses scarcely any

large ironclads, the only real war-vessels being sixteen monitors. There are a number of unarmoured steamers; but these would be of no service in modern warfare, for most of them are old craft, many, indeed, being former blockade-runners, fifty or sixty of which were seized during the war. We saw one of these lying at the wharf—an old Clyde-built paddle-steamer, such as was used years ago in the Highland or Irish coasting trade. Such boats, however, are often employed on survey duty, so they are not wholly valueless. The Americans are so secure in their isolated position that they need no navy to speak of: and, in the same way, their standing army consists of but twenty-five to thirty thousand men, and is used only to quell disturbances on the Indian frontier. During the civil war, the vast Federal and Confederate forces were composed of citizens who left their homes and their business to fight for the rival parties; and the consequence is, that nearly every middle-aged American you meet has his tale of battle and campaign. There are considerable militia regiments throughout the country.

The name "Arsenal" has a dignified ring; but the Washington Arsenal is just a great park, with a couple of large private houses and a few brick buildings. In the former reside the officers in authority; the latter are offices, and stores for war material. In the open park stand rows upon rows of dismounted guns—chiefly old fashioned and out of date, and endless piles of shot and shell, also old. It is an unspeakably happy thing for America that she does not require armaments like those of the European powers.

The United States' naval and military officers make Washington a sort of headquarters; and numbers of them may be seen about the city and in the hotels, mixing with the legislative crowd. It is hoped that Washington will in time become the fashionable resort of the States, where the *élite* of American society will gather during some part of the year, as Englishmen flock to London during the season. In some measure this has already begun; and wealthy Americans, not themselves connected with the legislature, are slowly commencing to build handsome residences in the city. If this plan can be carried out, we may see the waste places of Washington filled up with elegant private houses; otherwise the city is likely to remain bare, as it will never become a commercial centre.

Those persons whose practice in travelling is to "do" everything, will add to the noteworthy features of Washington the Corcoran Art Gallery, the Ordnance Museum, and the Smithsonian Institute. The Art Gallery consists of one room and a-half of paintings, with another room full of sculpture. Can the capital city of America not muster more pictures than this! The pictures are tolerably good, a number being by European artists. And in this connection it may be remarked, that the paintings to be found on the walls of American private houses are as a rule of an inferior class—often mere daubs. Surely here is an opening for some of our young artists whose work is good, but whose want of fame precludes their asking a high figure; there are hundreds of struggling artists in Britain who paint fairly, and yet are scarcely able to sell a third of their work, even at the lowest price. Their efforts are much superior to the productions referred to, which could hardly emanate from a respectable sign painter. And this fact the commonest powers of discrimination, even of the man who desires only to cover his wall at a certain contract price, could hardly fail to recognise.

The Ordnance Museum is small, but not without attraction; and the Smithsonian Institute and Museum is one of the inevitable rag and bone collections which one meets with everywhere.

The negro is very prominent in the population of Washington; and I had some talk with the hotel clerk about him. The clerk had fought in the Southern ranks during the war, and was therefore inclined to make out a case in favour of slavery. "General opinion, sir," he said, "has run dead against slavery; but I hold to the old way of things. It's all very well for the North and for outsiders to talk, but they know nothing about it. Down South we *live* among the blacks, and we can judge."

"Candidly, now, don't you think abolition has improved the negro? Isn't he rising in the social scale?"

"Certainly not. I am a Southerner, but I'm not so narrow-minded as to object to abolition if it really improved the black; but it don't. It may raise him a bit generations hence; but not in my lifetime, nor my son's either."

"But I hear great things about the aptitude of the black child to learn."

"That's all deceptive; the little blackguard shoots ahead wonderfully for a year or two, and then stops dead short. There's no bringing him past a certain point,—and that's a low one."

"Then what effect has abolition had in your experience?"

"It makes the beggars lazy and impudent; they've got the upper hand now, and they know it. They are not fit yet for elevation. And freedom has made them too thundering independent to learn!"

"I see a great number of negroes about the city, —are they employed as labourers, or what do they do?"

"Steal. That's all they do."

"Why, that's a very bad account. But they can't all live by stealing—they must do some sort of work."

"They do a job now and then just to keep them alive, but there's no steady work to be got out of them; whenever they've made anything, they leave off and go loafing around till necessity drives them back. Then their habits are disgusting,—they are so filthy, these villains, that they never touch water 'cept when it rains. And then they most go indoors till it's dry."

"Well now, take those black waiters, and the porters in the hall,—they seem a very decent lot. All I can say against them is, that they are too obliging! They rush to us on every pretence, and make a furious onset with a clothes-brush every time we leave the house."

"They are trained to that now, you see. And they are better than the rest; but still they're mighty stupid and obstinate. But we have a mortal bad crowd on the streets, big buck niggers that sneak up after dark in quiet places and will half murder you for the sake of your watch."

"Indeed? Well, we have seen a good deal of Washington streets at night, but never anything of that sort. I'm afraid you are prejudiced against the black fellows. Besides, if a nigger did attack you, he'd probably run away when you stood up to him."

"Not a bit of it. You can let ker-smash at a black fellow's head till you split your hand, and you won't hurt him;—you may knock him down a dozen times, but he's up again noways the worse. Their heads ain't like a white man's, they're too thundering thick for any created thing to hurt; I tell you that for a fact."

"Then what would you do if a nigger went for you?"

"Guess if I didn't shoot, I'd drive at his shins with my boot. Then you bet he'd howl, *and* scoot! They can't stand a kick on the shins."

At length we left Washington for Richmond, Virginia, having to rise at five A.M. to catch the train. It is a common thing in the States for trains—even when running short distances—to leave at unearthly hours; and it does not add to the convenience of travelling.

CHAPTER VII.

RICHMOND.

"THUNDER, what a bump! I say, conductor, do you lay the sleepers on top of the rails here? Immortal Cæsar, we're going sideways! No, it's only a somersault. Lookee here, conductor, just go 'long and tell the driver to let me know before he takes the next flying leap, so's I'll be ready, for blamed if I ain't split my coat and raised a two-inch patch off my scalp!"

"It is a bit roughish about here, I do say."

"Roughish! It's the meanest guess sort 'o track Eli G. Wilkins ever travelled, and that's my name, dry goods and general notion dealer, Columbus, Ohio!"

The road was rough, and we had not a good driver. He would start from every station with a shock that sent your heart into your mouth and your head against the panel,—then he would calm down a little and pick his way playfully over some loose stones,—then he would burst forth again into a wild ecstasy of jolts, and swing round a bad corner in a way that sent the life-blood shivering from your heart.

Then he would amble aimlessly up an incline, and tear down the other side like a misguided thunderbolt,—till eventually putting on full steam—and presumably sitting on the safety-valve—he would pull up short at the next station with a concussion that threatened to engulf passengers and train in sudden and irrevocable chaos. But by some mysterious chance, he brought us safely to Richmond, with no injury except to our feelings.

We wound along the bank of the Potomac for a long way, gazing at the broad frozen expanse, with here and there a black patch of open water, tenanted by wild ducks. The day was glorious, and the snow-covered country and frosted trees looked lovely glistening in the sun. America has winter scenes such as we do not know at home. Then, arrived in Richmond, we put up at the Exchange and Ballard, a queer rambling hotel thirty years old, and very like an old-fashioned English inn, consisting of two houses on opposite sides of the street, connected by a covered wooden passage.

Things down south seemed more homelike than farther north, if less luxurious. We had fires in the rooms, instead of the continual array of steam pipes used in the Northern States. But however cheery a fire may look, it does not diffuse the heat through a room like the steam apparatus. Accordingly, in the colder districts of America, and in Canada, the latter is always used, except in small houses and shanties, where a stove takes its place. The stove, though at first an abomination to the Briton, is soon found to be more effective than the open fireplace in preserving the temperature; but it generates a very dry close heat.

Richmond, like Rome, is built upon seven hills. They are not large hills; but they were a relief to us after the endless flat country. Every true Scotchman, after sojourning for some time on an unbroken plain, feels a woful dilapidation about the back muscles of his legs, and welcomes the very smallest hill, (for the sight of a hill is naturally synonymous with the desire to climb it).

Richmond is rather like a quiet English county town. It is aristocratic, and somewhat sleepy. In the lower parts it inclines to dirt and squalor. The black population seem to predominate over the white; and the negro stands out in his pristine splendour. Now, there are two distinct orders of negro. The first remains in the same social condition in which slavery left him, with apparently no desire to rise, and suggests a curious relic of the coal period, his native ebony shining through his rags, and surmounted by a venerable heirloom, which generations ago was a hat. The negro of the second class, on the other hand, has realized the importance of being "a man and a brudder," and marks his elevation by a swallow-tailed coat, a tasseled cane, and a scarf something between a rainbow and a flash of lightning. The necktie of the negro dandy is the most appalling piece of hosiery extant. Both orders wear a smile. But, though the negro has often a gigantic self-conceit, he has not, in the South at least, succeeded in inspiring the white man with respect. A tall Southerner, despatching a jet of tobacco juice towards the stove, remarked,—"They say the nigger's a man and a brother. Wall, I don't say he mayn't be somebody else's brother, but I reckon for sartin he ain't mine!"

The capitol of Richmond, the seat of the State Legislature, is a dismal square building, combining the less attractive features of a Methodist chapel and a gaol. In a small park surrounding it are statues of Washington, Henry Clay, and Stonewall Jackson. Henry Clay appears without the cigar which is commonly attributed to him, and which so widely bears his name; so we assume the effigy to be a misrepresentation. The statue of Jackson is a gift from English gentlemen, in token of their appreciation of the man. A number of English gentlemen have long been resident in the neighbourhood.

The South claims for itself "bluer blood" and a longer pedigree than the North. There are a number of old English families settled in the Southern States, and a number of estates held by country gentlemen. In the North, the country gentleman or large landed proprietor is unknown, and the absence of such a class is a distinct want. Every one is in business, and remains so till late in life. Even then, if a man retires with a fortune, he spends his time and his money between the city and the fashionable watering place; he has no thought of buying an estate. His tastes have not led him to expect happiness from such a course, for out of the whirl of city society he would be isolated and unhappy. Now those Northern States of America, with their rare commercial energy, and their remarkable progress in all things practical, stand much in need of a counterbalancing influence. Though practice be excellent, it is possible to be too practical. The Northern States are as yet one-sided; they want a class composed of men of leisure, who will give their time to the advancement of art and refinement, and tend to tone the nation. The country gentleman, from the peculiar advantages of his position, is the man required.

Now, in thus asserting the want of a landed class in the North, we cannot affirm the South to possess much superiority. There is the country gentleman in the South, but he is not the true sort. He wants energy. He may be high-spirited, hospitable, and honourable; but he is a drone. Assure him of his yearly income, give him a table at which to entertain his friends, and he is content. He is the good-hearted easy-going idler, seated in his cane chair with a cigar and a bottle of wine; but he is not the true energetic country gentleman, giving up his time to refining pursuits and the social welfare and elevation of his people. And this pernicious state of things in the South has beyond question been induced by slavery.

Virginia and Maryland are known to be the chief tobacco-producing states of the Union; and Richmond is full of tobacco factories. In the course of our explorations we turned into one of these, and saw the process of preparing the leaf. The price of raw tobacco leaf, as bought by the manufacturer, ranges from as low as two cents to one dollar per pound. The finer quality of leaf is sweetened by soaking in sugar and liquorice; the coarser is steeped in sugar and molasses. In the very purest tobacco there is ten per cent. of sweetening material, and in inferior kinds the latter may amount to forty or fifty per cent. Negroes are employed in the factories; and it was a curious sight to see these fellows plunging the leaf into the sweetening compound. Physically they were a splendid set, and being stripped to the waist, their long brawny arms and black herculean chests glistened with the molasses, like the wrestlers of old lubricated for the Olympic games. The tobacco in general use in the States is very hot, and not at first suited to the British palate (though the Londoner who smokes bird's eye might not complain of it); but not until we reached Canada did we get a really satisfactory pipe.

If tobacco is cheap in America, Havana cigars are not. The import duty is about 14s. per lb., and the real Havana stands at about double English prices. Unmanufactured leaf is, however, imported from Havana at a duty of only 1s. 6d. per lb.; and cigars made within the States of this Havana leaf are sold everywhere at moderate prices—at least they bear the name of Havana leaf, for not one in four has any resemblance to the genuine article. The American home manufactured or domestic cigar is "cabbagy," and much to be avoided.

A good deal of flour, made from Virginia wheat, is milled in Richmond, principally for export to the South American market. Cheap means of transport is afforded by the James River, upon which the city is built, and which is deep enough for traders of three or four hundred tons.

The country round about Richmond is pleasantly sprinkled with thick pine woods, with here and there a farmhouse or private residence peeping out; while the soil is very red, and excellent for wheat growing. We were surprised to see the past season's corn stalks standing to a height of two or three feet; and found that the corn is not cut down as at home, but only husked. It was our first sight of the American corn stalk, and very strange it seemed—an inch thick, and more like a hemlock or reed than a cornstalk. Here and there among the corn-fields appeared traces of the war, in grass-grown rifle trenches and flanking batteries, many of them in perfect preservation.

The hall of the Exchange and Ballard Hotel was a great "loafing" centre. And the hotel clerks seemed to be quite on an equality with their customers, dining with them at table d'hôte, and sitting in the hall smoking and chatting like old friends. Many of the clerks of southern hotels are young men of good family, who "came down" during the war, which may account in great measure for this state of things. Then a good many of the townspeople would drop into the hotel of an evening to see what was going on. This was the nightly style of thing in the hall.

Scene—a huge stove, surrounded by a variety of

cane chairs thrown back on their hind legs, each containing a long-legged occupant—clerks included. Enter a new-comer, rubbing his hands.

"Evening, lads! Mighty cold, ain't it? Any one got a lucifer?"

Receives the match, ignites it on his trouser, and lights up.

"Come any luck hunting last Toosday, Will?"

(My friend Davis, being of horsey proclivities, pricks up his ears).

"Why no. Four quail and a duck. Dog tracked a deer some ways, but lost the scent down to Jones's creek."

"Hunting!" gasps Davis. "Do you call that hunting! Why, that's shooting."

"Shooting? Well, I reckon it's much the same,—we call all sport hunting. But you mean fox-hunting, like in England; well, we have that too, when there ain't frost. Frost will be clearing away pretty speedy now, for it never lasts beyond a week here; and there's a fox-meet fixed for middle of next week. Reckon you'll stay *and* ride?"

"I should like to uncommonly; but we'll have to leave in two days, I'm afraid."

"Ah! that's unlucky. For we do have a nice country hereabouts for riding, *and* lively foxes. Fond of duck and quail hunting?"

" Of shooting ? Yes, pretty well. You ought to have a lot of duck down by the river, I should say."

" Creeks are just swarming with them, if you can get nigh enough."

" You have no game-laws in the States, have you ? "

" No, you just take your fowling-piece and go right where you please, so long as you don't damage any man's property. But we have close seasons for the game."

Enter a friend, who proposes a drink. All adjourn to the bar, with a subsequent view to billiards; except a big Virginian, who, having got the best chair, is disinclined to vacate it.

" And so you are from England, gentlemen. Well now, that's a place I'd like to visit, for we've a mighty kind feelin' to the old country, down South here. I'm English myself; leastways my grandfather came from there. From Nottingham about, I think it was. Pike's my name—maybe you'll have met some of our folks in England ? "

"Well, you see, England's a biggish place. Besides, we are Scotch."

" Scotch ! Ah then, you'll not likely have heard of our people."

" I suppose you had pretty hard times here during the war. Were you in it ? "

" I reckon there's scarce a man in Richmond City

that wasn't out against these Northern skunks. And we had a sight of Englishmen with us too. It was a mean fight that, I tell you! Slavery! these Yankees said;—it wasn't slavery at all they wanted to fight about—it was jest the spite they had against us, and jealousy; and the Irish, and Germans, and thieves they brought down with them cared for nought but to plunder. They—"

"Stop a bit. As to slavery, I want to hear what you say about that. You know that though you had a good many Englishmen in your ranks, they were not fighting to uphold slavery;—we don't believe in that in Britain?"

"Well, I dunno that I'd go to uphold slavery. I would say the new way is better for us. It's cheaper sartinly. A black man's labour in the fields costs about 150 dollars a year now, and he keeps his own wife and family. Before the war there were allus old slaves about the place past workin', and young children too, and that would bring the yearly cost of a workin' nigger up to nigh 250 dollars. But I say the nigger himself was better cared for then than he is now."

"That might be so in the case of humane slave-owners—but how many such were there!"

"They were most of em' good to the niggers. For it paid them best to treat them well. The nigger was no ways so badly off as the North went to say he was."

"Why did the planters ever begin to bring slaves over? Why couldn't they hire white labourers?"

"No white man could stand workin' in the plantations in the heat. Now you'll see these black fellows often workin' barehead in the blazin' sun."

"But you can't deny that the slaves were often treated shamefully. The cruelty of some owners must have been horrible."

"Well, and haven't I said I'd never uphold that? I don't go along with cruelty to the nigger at all. But you can take your oath of this—that there's no way but floggin' to punish them; it's the only way to make 'em feel. They don't mind anythin' else. And you'll believe that's so, when I say it's the way they punish them now in the State prisons; it's the law."

"How do the blacks get along now with those who used to be their masters? Is there not any ill-feeling for past wrongs?"

"I tell you there weren't near so many wrongs as you say. And the nigger's jest much as he allus was, kinder childlike and harmless,—but mortal lazy. And he'll allus be."

CHAPTER VIII.

A LONG JOURNEY, AND A SQUALLING BABY.

A THOUSAND miles by rail! That was the prospect that lay before us on the morning we left Richmond. Chicago was our bourne; and we meant to go straight through, traversing the States of Virginia and Ohio on our way, a journey of forty-eight hours. We were obliged, however, to stay the afternoon at Washington, proceeding thence by the night train. Although we had to travel over more than one line of railway, we were able at Richmond to purchase tickets for the whole distance, the respective companies adjusting such matters between themselves.

That part of the road leading over the Alleghany mountains is picturesque—and badly ballasted. We passed through this region during the night, and were therefore prevented from rendering to the scenery its due meed of admiration; but we had ample opportunity to prove the roughness of the running. Such a violent swaying and shaking is there, indeed, that it is no uncommon thing for people to be "seasick." After a tolerable sleep in the Pullman berths, we went out on the snow covered car platform for ten minutes to freshen up. It is a strange sensation to stand on the back platform of the last car, with the train doing forty miles down an incline, and feel the snow whirling up in a mist round about you, while you watch the two black rails rushing from beneath till they converge to a point on the white track far behind. "You need to stick right close to the railing with one hand, and hold your hair on with the other," as an American finely observed.

Two of our companions principally attracted us, both of them Chicago men, and we beguiled the time with sundry rubbers of whist. One of these gentlemen had a particularly high opinion of his own play, and favoured his partner with instructions at every turn of the game. He professed to hold closely to the rules laid down by Hoyle; but the fact was that he proceeded on a system entirely his own.

"My dear sir," he would say to Davis, who played with him, "you shouldn't have played that king of spades second in hand."

"But I had only the king and a small one."

"Never mind, sir; it was bad play. Upon no occasion play your king second."

Again—

"Why did you take that trick, sir? You should have left it to me; I would have taken it."

"Well, as you had trumped my best card twice in succession, and had evidently nothing to bring in when you did get the lead, I thought I might as well take the chance of bringing in my diamonds."

"False play again, sir—very false play. You should have left it to me."

At last Davis could stand it no longer. Our friend had taken no notice whatever of a twice repeated lead in trump; and Davis, laying down his hand, said impressively,

"Mr Schultz, do you know what the Paisley man said to his partner who wouldn't return him trumps?"

"No."

"It was this:—'There are only two occasions on which it is excusable not to return your partner's lead in trumps. The one is—if you haven't any; the other, if you are struck dead on the spot!'"

"He did, did he? A—h! Well, that isn't Hoyle."

"Whether it's Hoyle or not, I'm not in a position to say; but it's WHIST! Let me impress that on you."

Davis was a good player, and Mr Schultz's vagaries had nearly driven him wild.

The American's knowledge of whist is generally speaking small. However excellent at "poker" or "seven up," he can seldom approach an Englishman at the king of games.

Apart from cards, Mr Schultz was a most amusing companion, and a good specimen of the better class American of the present day. He was Brother Jonathan out and out, and yet not that very exaggerated Brother Jonathan whom good folks are inclined to believe in at home. All Americans do not speak broadly through their noses, nor address you as "old hoss;" they do not "darn their eyes," nor make repeated reference in ordinary conversation to the Star-spangled Banner and the Cause of Freedom. The vividly typical American of the past has died out; or rather is to be found only among the middle and lower orders. (The latter certainly display their nationality very clearly.) But the American of the better class is nevertheless easily distinguishable by the observant Englishman; just as the Englishman is unmistakeable by the American. He possesses the old typical features, but they are much subdued; he has a fine nasal twang, but it is delicately softened; he uses a good many Americanisms in conversation, but they are not offensive; and there are points about his dress which, though slight, are yet peculiarly American.

"Are you going through the whole way?" Schultz inquired.

"Straight on to Chicago.'

"Ah now, that's pleasant, because we shall be fellow-travellers. Have you ever been in Chicago before?"

"No, this is our first time."

"Really! I calculate then it won't be your last. When you have been there once, you'll want to go back again."

"You are evidently a Chicago man, then?"

"Well, I've been doing business there for nine years, and I don't feel like leaving now. There's an attraction in the place; it's so lively that you would feel any other city pretty much slow in comparison. Everything is moving along—trade always keen, and for amusement in the evenings, a—h!"

"It was wonderful the way you pulled up after the fire."

"It was. But you have only heard of it. Now you ought to have seen it. I was there; and it was the queerest sight in life to go through the streets right after. The merchants didn't stop and begin whining, I tell you; but each man just raised a board shed right away on top of the ashes for the bit of goods he'd got left, and nailed up a shingle saying he was there to receive orders and go straight on as if nothing had happened."

"They must have been plucky fellows, I must say!"

"Yes, sir. Just before the fire you might have parted with a man in his elegant private room, in a store so large that it took a whole block for itself;—two days after, you would see that same man sitting on a box-end among the ruins, with nothing left but his iron safe, writing up his books on the head of a cask, and looking as cheerful and settled as if he'd been there all his life."

"It must have been a grand time for the thieves and blackguards of the place!"

"Not so much as you'd have thought. You see every man kept a peculiar spry look-out on his effects; and whenever he saw a loafer clearing off with any article, he'd just nip out the pop-gun and let him have it in the rear. And the loafers didn't most like that. I remember—Jehoshaphat! there's that hollering infant again!"

There was a squalling child in the carriage, which proved a most disturbing element, and with which Schultz was on terms of bitter hostility.

"What a pity, now," said Schultz shortly after, "that you hadn't been travelling in summer. You get no sort of idea of the country just now, and it is really pretty round here."

"It seems very roughly cultivated anyhow; and I haven't seen a decent farm-house,—they are all wretched little log cabins."

"It is mainly owned by small squatters, and they are apt to get lazy at times, for—"

Boo—hoo—hoo! from the baby.

"The afflicted Moses!—You see it don't take these squatters much trouble to grow as much as will give them their daily bread, and then they're content. But we come to a good farming district when we strike the Ohio."

Boo—hoo—hoo—hoo—!

Here Schultz made a fearful face at the baby, which forthwith went into hysterics; and the father, catching Mr Schultz's expression, looked sternly at him.

"Fine healthy child that, sir," says Schultz, to cover his confusion. "And quite a *re*markable power of voice. I should say, now, he's all lungs together! Guess he can't have room inside for much else."

Father, relaxing—"Well, he is a strong boy, if he's a bit noisy. Fond of children, sir?"

"Oh, uncommon! Tell you what, now," says Schultz demoniacally, "I think the little one is troubled with the heat. It's only fresh air he wants. I'd take him on to the platform a spell, if I were you."

Afflicted parents catch at the idea, and disappear outside. Fiendish exultation on the part of Schultz, and period of temporary quiet.

"I guess I played it on them there!" says Schultz.

But our interval of peace was shortlived. Five minutes brought back parents and child, blue and shivering, the baby yelling like a steam whistle.

Boo—hoo—hoo—hoo—hoo! Boo—hoo—hoo—oo!

It began to get serious. Schultz waxed grimly sarcastic, and addressed the unhappy father.

"There's a quiet pathos, sir, about that infant, that is deeply interesting. He shows early signs of a fine susceptibility."

"Wish he warn't so blamed susceptible."

"Not at all, sir; you are quite wrong. These are indications of character. Something has appealed to his feelings, and he wants to give it expression. Now sir, you shouldn't let that talent be lost. There's a power of eloquence about that child—you must develop it. I would recommend his being trained either for the pulpit or the auction-box."

We went on for half an hour, the baby going from bad to worse. Blandishments, threats, sugar-candy, and expostulations were expended with no effect. Schultz said nothing, but the terrible workings of his soul were visible in his face. He was revolving some dire project in his mind. At last he brightened. He leaned over to me and whispered—"I've struck it now. Watch me fix the little cuss!"

The parents had laid the child on the seat in despair, and were gazing blankly at each other. Schultz extracted a plug of chewing tobacco from his waistcoat pocket, and seizing his opportunity, stealthily conveyed it into the baby's hand. The baby, as a natural consequence, inserted it in its mouth—without its guardians' knowledge. Schultz smiled a fearful smile. Soon the baby grew calm, and the parents looked triumphantly round the carriage. Schultz appeared buried in thought. All at once an exclamation was heard. A brown stream was trickling from the infant's lips,—the mother rushed at it, opened its mouth, and produced the "quid." Parents horror-struck; Schultz moved with deep and active sympathy. Presently symptoms appeared, necessitating the child's removal to the window; Schultz still manifesting the utmost concern. Eventually the baby was drawn in in a state of collapse, and soon afterwards went to sleep from sheer internal exhaustion.

"Wherever could it have got it?" says the father, in dreadful agitation.

"Horrible!" says Schultz, "horrible! It's awful to think of. It might have swallowed it. Infants are so innocent, they'd eat most anything. What a mercy you found it in time!"

"It must have been laying around upon the seat."

"So it must. Of course. Shocking of any man to

leave tobacco about in that way; there's no saying what might have happened." Then turning to me when the commotion had subsided,—

" I said I'd settle the little cuss. *And I have!*"

However indefensible the means, the effect was undoubted. The baby was effectually silenced, and finished the journey in a state of coma, while peace was secured to the car. I merely throw out the suggestion, that Winslow's Soothing Syrup might find a formidable rival in Virginia Chewing Tobacco.

We came upon the upper part of the Ohio at Benwood, and found the river closed with ice, so that steamers had ceased running for the winter. In summer, the steamers on these great continental streams afford a most pleasant means of locomotion, much more desirable, if slower, than the train.

We arrived in Chicago early on the third morning, after two days and two nights on the rail, drove to the Palmer House, and luxuriated in a wash. Nothing (with the exception perhaps of chimney sweeping), has the same effect as railway travelling in inducing dirt. It is a curious ethnological fact, that the Anglo-Saxon is the only man known really to enjoy cold water. Coming in from a journey, no matter how hungry he is, he goes directly for a wash; while a German or other foreigner, no matter how dirty he is, first satisfies the cravings of his appetite.

The Palmer House is a magnificent hotel, situated on the principal thoroughfare of Chicago; so that the look-out from the sitting room windows is always cheerful. American hotels have usually a ground floor of shops, with their principal rooms immediately above; and the elevation is quite a coign of vantage from which to survey the street. The Palmer House is immense; it has seven hundred visitors' rooms; it cost £450,000 to build, and £100,000 to furnish. Everything is on a colossal scale, everything is first class,—and the daily board is only twelve shillings.

CHAPTER IX.

SOMETHING ABOUT CHICAGO.

Soon after our arrival the weather became very severe, and varied for three days from twenty to twenty-six degrees below zero. Added to the frost there was a strong wind, which, rising in the distant regions of the icy north-west, and sweeping without check for hundreds of miles over the level prairie, swooped in gusts round the street corners, and bit to the very bone. A "cold snap," as it is called, like this, seldom lasts long, and everyone who can keeps within doors during its continuance; while such unhappy ones as have to be abroad, appear in fur caps with ear-flaps closely tied down, and hurry as if for very life. A public man can pursue his way along the street at such a season without fear of being "button-holed:" and a Chicago nor'-wester in winter time has more effect in inducing people to "move on," than all the adjurations of a score of policemen.

In the midst of this intense frost, the Post Office, a great square block of building, was burnt to the ground. Fifteen or twenty steam fire-engines were upon the scene, but proved of little avail, for the streams of water directed at the upper windows broke into spray and froze in the air, rendering the hose virtually useless. The firemen were cased in waterproofs and sou'-westers, and looked like moving masses of ice. All firemen had need of a fearless spirit, but these men doubly so,—for walking on a seventy feet wall covered with ice wherever the fire leaves the smallest space, is considerably worse than our firemen's work, bad as that is; but the Chicago brigade acquitted themselves nobly, in the teeth of all the danger and hardship. Now and then a man in working the hose got his hands covered with ice, and required to be taken to a neighbouring house to have them melted; while many were frost bitten.

It is worthy of note as a sample of American energy, that on the very afternoon of the fire, the entire postal staff were settled at work in temporary premises,—the necessary alterations made on those premises, and not a mail was missed! And the General Post Office of a commercial city of 500,000 inhabitants is no puny establishment.

Chicago still shows a strong partiality for fires; and hardly a day passed without our hearing the warning bell, and seeing the engines go tearing past. The people proceed upon the principle that cure is better than prevention, and have organised a very efficient brigade service. They take a laudable pride in this body, and are pleased to see it provided with suitable opportunities for exercise.

A heavy fall of snow coming on, the whole city turned out in sleighs. There was every variety of sleigh, from the trim cutter or light sleigh for two, to the heavy omnibus and the goods waggon. Many of the latter simply had their wheels taken off for the winter, and runners substituted. The horses of the lighter vehicles all wore bells, to give warning of their approach ; for the sleighs come on so swiftly and silently, that accidents would otherwise occur. Each private sleigh is furnished with furs or buffalo robes, which hang over the back, and almost sweep the ground. The scene from the lofty hotel window down upon the street, with its stream of sleighs skimming past in both directions, was to us most novel and animated.

Having friends in Chicago, we submitted ourselves to their direction, and were conducted among the wonders of the place. *The* feature of Chicago is its marvellous energy. America is energetic, but Chicago is in a fever. It does not rest one moment, but goes on, on—ever ceaselessly ahead—to buying, and selling, and getting gain. Everything is rapid, everything is keen. There are hardly any idlers on the streets. Everyone has an object in immediate view,—and is walking fast to reach it. The great trade is, of course, Western produce. Grain, flour, live stock, dead meat, hams, wild duck, prairie hen, quails, butter, cheese, and vegetables come pouring daily in from the vast Western country, to be sent forth again to the Eastern States and the world at large. Chicago is the great mart of the West, the centre to which all supplies converge. It might almost be called the butcher's and grocer's shop of the world. Manufactured goods, again, such as cloths and hardware, are imported into the city from the East, and distributed to the surrounding country in return for its produce. Our friend of the ocean steamer had not exaggerated greatly after all, in proclaiming the marvels of Chicago. For mercantile enterprise, it stands alone, the most remarkable city of the world.

Our cicerone led us along Market Street, and down Water Street, where each shop is a provision store. The stores seemed too small for their contents; for the very pavement was crowded with carcases of hogs, deer, and rabbits, all frozen stiff as stone. Of course, such a state of things could not obtain during the heat of summer. We went into a small store, and watched an American bargain. Everything is in a free and easy style,—which curiously does not seem to detract from the sharpness and real attention to business. The salesman in this place held an apple in one hand, which he munched continuously, while he rapidly cast up accounts with the other. Presently in came a customer, who went straight to the apple barrel, and likewise supplied himself. Not a word had passed as yet. The customer began to poke round among some tubs of butter.

Customer—with his back to salesman, and an air of unconcern—

Munch—munch—munch. "Mornin." Munch munch. "I'll take sixty tubs Choice Dairy at ten-and-a-half cents."

Salesman—

"Calculate you will! Price is eleven-a-half." Munch—munch.

"Eleven-a-half! I had eighty tubs yesterday from Smart & Reilly at ten a-quarter." Munch—munch —munch.

"Guess you'd best try Smart & Reilly again." Munch.

"Say ten three-quarters, and I'll trade." Munch— Munch.

"No, you don't." Munch.

Customer, turning to face him—

"Eleven?"

"Scarcely." Munch.

"Wall, we can't close." (Indifferently). Munch— munch. Selects another apple, and moves to the door.

Salesman—

"Say!"

"Ah?"

"*And* a-quarter.   Eleven a-quarter?"

"Write it down.   Delivery by three o'clock." Munch, and exit.

(This, it may be well to remark, is not the universal style of doing business in large houses).

We visited the principal dry goods warehouses, several of these being of extraordinary proportions. In one of them alone there was lying a stock worth £300,000, despite its being the dull season of the year. These wholesale establishments are known in the States as "jobbing" houses; the word thus having, in America, an exactly opposite signification to what it has at home.

A large boot and shoe factory engaged our attention, where everything was done by machinery. To prove the celerity of the process of manufacture, the manager offered to take our measure, and have a pair of boots begun and finished in seventeen minutes! We would willingly have gratified him, but did not happen to be in need of pedal integuments at that juncture; and besides—the boots on show frightened us. It was not that they were of bad material—their stuff and workmanship were excellent; but their shape,—their unspeakable shape! The present fashion of American boot is short and squat, with broad square toes and high heels. It seems modelled on a system of straight lines; for we could find no curve in the article to speak of. The upper end culminates in a leather leg, like an English Wellington. " Boots," in America, always mean Wellingtons; "shoes" stand for ordinary lacing boots; and if you want a pair of shoes, you must refer to them as "ankle shoes," and will probably require to give an illustration. The free and enlightened citizen buys his boots ready made; hence they are made on an invariable scale of sizes, distinguished by numbers. He does not crave the luxury of a boot made specially to fit the foot; he reverses the order, and makes the foot fit the boot. Certainly he does but little walking, always taking a car when he can; and may not therefore feel the same need for a well-fitting boot as the pedestrian Briton. The American uses his boot for sitting in; and for purposes of contemplation. He generally so disposes his legs that his boots may be within easy range of his eyes; and then he gazes at them in pleased reverie. He has usually small neat feet, in which he takes a pride; and the peculiar thing is, that he considers his national boot a masterpiece of St Crispin's art! In New York and Boston, the Englishman may get a proper boot as at home; but not, I regret to say, in the West.

In the factory referred to, the coarser descriptions of boots are made by convict labour, which Government allows at seventeen pence per day; so that artisans are employed in the manufacture of the finer kinds only. This system of employing convict labour at so low a rate as to preclude honest workmen from competing, is naturally in great disfavour with the workmen.

Chicago is built upon a swamp, but it nevertheless enjoys a good reputation for health. Some of the streets are laid with wood, and sound quite hollow when carriages pass over them, thus shewing the nature of the ground below. The streets are broad, but not too broad for the traffic. The business part of the city looked more like a solid Scotch town than any other place we visited; the buildings are of stone, substantial and rather handsome; and there are no mean tumble-down houses to mar the beauty of the principal thoroughfares, as in New York; for when rebuilding the city after the fire, the Chicago people did the thing well.

Situated on the southern shore of Lake Michigan, and with a spreading network of railway communication, Chicago possesses the most signal facilities for trade. No more suitable spot could have been selected for the great headquarters of Western merchandise. We walked hither and thither among the docks and along the shore of the lake, which has exactly the appearance of the sea, no land being visible on the horizon. The harbour has a breakwater about a mile long, with lighthouses like any seaport. On the wharves we passed through piles upon piles of lumber cut into deals, lying in readiness for shipment; the famous Michigan pine lumber being shipped principally from this port. Down by the lake stand the City Waterworks, containing a gigantic steam engine for pumping in water from the lake, which is considered one of the sights of Chicago.

A bustling citizen met me one morning in the hall of the hotel, and seeing my nationality, opened fire without delay.

" Morning, sir, Just arrived ? "

" Well, not very long since. I came here three days ago."

" Ah ! And what house, may I ask, do you represent ? "

" I beg your pardon ? "

" What house—what commercial establishment ? What class of goods are you pushing ? "

" I'm not travelling on business."

" Not—on—business ! " Gasps. Then quickly recovering himself—" Ah ; going to settle. Looking around for a spot, I *pre*sume ? "

"Scarcely that either. In fact, I'm ashamed to own that I'm merely on pleasure."

"Pleasure! is that so? But with a view to future business;—doubtless. Here's my card, sir—'John T. Smithson—hardware—Monroe Street!' You find this a smart city, sir?"

"Keen enough, in all conscience. You don't seem to feel the dull times here as we do in Britain?"

"We've had our spell of them, you be certain; but things are lifting now. Resumption of specie payments is promoting confidence."

"That was a much needed step."

"It was. A man couldn't tell till this Janu*airy* what the dollar might be worth a week ahead. But now we are withdrawing the balloon paper issues, and confidence is returning. A gold basis, sir, means commercial prosperity."

"It ought, anyhow, to mean a considerable cheapening in prices."

"Yes; they'll settle down to a steadier figure. Then, since last fall, men don't care to become bankrupts."

"That is a happy state of things. How does it come to be?"

"Why, the old system was repealed then, and a man can't claim his legal discharge now till he dies :— or pays his debts."

"That must make a considerable difference in

commercial circles. You will have fewer failures now, I should say?"

"Yes, sirree. Now, I'll tell you—the number of men who took advantage of the old act, just before it was repealed, was *a* circumstance. In one day, sir, in this city of Chicago, four hundred men went into bankruptcy!"

"A healthy state of things, I must say! Caused by speculation, I suppose?"

"Yes, sir. Every man started to make a bigger show than his neighbour, and spent above his means;—speculated, and got busted."

"Indeed! I thought that form of vanity was confined to England; I thought that in this free and independent country, especially in the West, a man didn't care what his neighbour thought of him, and didn't want to outshine in private life?"

"Well, a man mightn't care much,—but you bet his wife did! It's the women that most run a man to folly here. Guess you don't see me hitched up like that."

"How do you mean?"

"I guess you don't see me rushing into matri*mony*. No, sir, I'm mighty comfortable now; I spend my three thousand dollars every year, and I can afford it; but a wife would smash me. I'm aware when I'm thriving."

"Rather a disappointment for the ladies, Mr Smithson!"

"Well; it may be so. Perhaps it is. Now I have two brothers; one of 'em's married to a young lady in this city—he's got just thirty-five hundred dollars a year, and she's been spending six thousand. She'll clean him out in another twelvemonth, so that he won't have a red cent left. I've warned him, but t'ain't no use; he's blind as a board fence. Then the other one has gone and engaged himself:—but he's a smart lad, if he is a bit young,—and he's struck money. Daughter of the largest wholesale grocery house in the city." (Pensively) "Yes; Nathan always was a smart lad!"

"You might follow his example."

"I might; and yet I guess I won't. You see I have a boss time now, everything I want, and no worry. My mother used to tell me (she was from Hartland, Maine, and a woman of uncommon sense), —she used to tell me, when I was a boy;—'John T., you be industrious and careful, and stick to business. Don't go foolin' with the girls, but live sober and sensible till you're forty: and then if you must have a wife, don't go for looks, but marry a plain woman that can bake apple puddins', and she'll make you a happy home.' I've held to her words for thirty-five years, and I calculate she was main right. Ah, there's the gentleman I'm looking for; guess I'll bid you good morning."

I was considerably staggered. Was the man a fool, that he selected an utter stranger to entrust with his domestic history? Hardly; his appearance denoted prosperity and dollars, and his face lacked nothing of shrewdness. He was not·one whom his fellow-men would single out of the crowd to borrow money from, or on whom to play a practical joke. But this easy confidence is in America no unusual national trait. A casual acquaintance of ten minutes' standing will often make you the recipient of a lengthy confidence, giving you a full account of his income and yearly expenditure, and going on to discuss his prospects of marriage, or his eldest child's recovery from whooping-cough. To the self-contained Briton it is at first very strange. And the man who thus lays bare his family concerns appears to have no ulterior object, for he seldom seeks any confidence in return; he talks from the pure love of conversation. America is a great country; but peculiar,—very peculiar!

CHAPTER X.

SOMETHING MORE ABOUT CHICAGO.

"WHAT did you pay for those boots?"

The speaker was a specimen of young America, whom we had noticed every night in the smoking-room of the Palmer House. He used to sit for hours in one arm-chair, with his feet upon another, and his hat tilted over his forehead; while he employed his whole brain power in the conduct of a pipe. He had surveyed us for several evenings in attentive silence, till he at last broke the ice with the words—

"What did you pay for those dress boots?"

"My boots? About twenty-five shillings."

"Twenty-five shillings. That will be six dollars and a quarter. My! but that was cheap. You got them in Europe?"

"I did. Why, what do you pay for the same here?"

"They'd run twelve dollars in Chicago. And what would be the cost of that tweed suit you're wearing?"

"Four guineas. That's twenty-one dollars of your money."

"You'd be charged fifty dollars here. What do you say, now, that this overcoat cost me?"

He took up rather a nice heavy overcoat which was lying beside him.

"I don't know. In England you would get it for four pound ten or thereabouts."

"Forty-five dollars, sir. I guess there's a difference."

"Forty-five dollars! The thing is awful. But do you mean to say you can't get those things any cheaper?"

"Not if you go to the first-class stores. There's plenty of cheap clothing to be had in the city; but it ain't good, and it don't fit. If you want to dress nicely, you must go to the best stores."

"And what is the reason of those enormous prices?"

"Well, wages are high; and then the best clothing is all English goods."

"Ah—your import duties again;—a nice bugbear they are to this land of freedom! Why, your clothes are just cent. per cent. dearer than ours! You would require to have a good income. But I suppose they pay clerks in offices and warehouses better here than in England?"

"I'm twenty-one now, and I've been in a dry goods store four years, and I get seven hundred dollars."

"A hundred and forty pounds ;—there it is, you see. You can afford it pretty well, for living is cheap on this side."

"Board ain't high ; but you take your oath I spend all I make, and no trouble to do it either. Still I'm not hard to content. If I can get good clothes to wear, good tobacco to smoke, and good food to eat, I calculate I don't look for more, either in this world or the next. But I do like good living."

"You do, eh ?"

"*I* tell you, sir. Guess you'll always find me *there* at meal times. I'm death on my food. I'd be ready for a square meal most any time of the day."

He emphasised this strongly, and was evidently an unconscionable young glutton.

"Do you know that over here people eat far too much? You are always eating; and you mix your food in a most appalling way."

"Too much! Why, I'm never satisfied! I like this hotel now: they give you a handsome meal in the restaurant for forty cents; and they do make elegant pie. I'm wonderful fond of pie."

"There it is again—you are always stuffing with pies and sweets in this country. Why can't you stick to something solid?"

"Don't know; but I'm main fond of pie."

"I have gone into refreshment rooms on the railways, and found nothing but pies and pastry; I could hardly get a decent meat sandwich. It's very sad to see men spoiling themselves with pie in that wholesale way."

"Well; I like pie. And you do get elegant pie in this restaurant."

"Do you live in the hotel?"

"I have a room near by that I sleep in; but I always come here for meals, and I stop here evenings, unless I go to the theatre."

"Then you don't live with your family?"

"They stop down in Hartford, Connecticut; and I'm here in the store."

"Why man, you have no idea of comfort; you are a regular vagrant. You ought to have a lodging of your own, and make it as much like home as possible; it's out of sight better to have your beer and your pipe in your own rooms than to go loafing every night about a hotel."

"Well, I guess this suits me. I'm quite happy."

"What do you do on summer evenings and holidays? Do you go in for sport, or walking, or cricket, or athletics?"

"Scarcely: no sir, I guess not. If I want amusement, I go to the theatre. That's lively;—now that's what I call fun."

And thus our conversation closed. I left my young friend in his arm-chair, lazily puffing; and if the reader of this should ever chance to enter the Palmer House smoking-room, I have no doubt he will find him puffing there still!

Now this youth represents a large class of young America. He had this peculiarity certainly, that he seemed to have few companions, whereas the average American youth has no lack of them; but in other respects he was a fair sample of his class. Their creed is, "Work hard during the day, and enjoy yourself in the evening"— a fair creed, if the second part be rightly interpreted. The first maxim they act up to; American lads work well, and work late and early; they seem to throw their whole mind into business during business hours. But their idea of enjoyment outside the warehouse is often feeble; they do not care for healthy exercise, nor for those pastimes which develop the body and strengthen the constitution for the day's labour,—they rather look down on these as unworthy of their years, and would feel out of place in a football jersey or in cricketing flannels. It is a more manly thing to hang round a hotel bar-room, or frequent a music-hall. A pernicious way of things has sprung up of late. American parents live much in hotels, and their families do not know real domestic life; then the children are pampered and encouraged, and led to consider themselves men and women at thirteen. The system is bad. There is a wide difference between angelic precocity and impish forwardness. The American child is precocious to offensiveness. The American boy of fifteen is thought old enough to direct his own tastes, is lavishly supplied with pocket money, and naturally tends to cigars and billiards. The American city boy is taught not to soil his clothes, and avoids such games as might eventuate in a patch of mud or a torn jacket; accordingly, he has to seek artificial outlet for his boyish spirits, and lands in fields not so green and pastures not so innocent. He is unhappy away from a good restaurant or a theatre. The country boy, again, is very much the same as any ordinary boy; and has therefore a fair chance of becoming a good man. But the city lad is badly trained, and heavily handicapped at the start in the race for a healthy, natural life.

We visited the famous Chicago Stock Yards; where the cattle brought in from the surrounding country are collected, killed, and prepared for export. The Stock Yards are within the city limits, but nevertheless six miles distant from the Palmer House, which is in the heart of the city. Chicago, like most recent American cities, has been laid out in view of future growth, and the distances are very great. The Stock Yards form a vast square enclosure, perhaps a mile and a half each way; while within are innumerable pens for hogs and cattle, and a number of slaughter and packing houses, each belonging to a different business firm. The odour is hardly that of Araby the blest. Railway lines bring the stock into the centre of the enclosure, and take out the hams and beef. Fifty thousand hogs are thus killed and converted into hams in twenty-four hours in several of the larger establishments; everything, except the actual slaughtering process, being done by machinery. The Stock Yards are not agreeable, but they are very wonderful.

The herdsmen in charge of the larger cattle work on horseback, and have dogs like rough colleys, while they carry heavy stockwhips. Like most Western prairie men, they ride entirely by balance, swinging with every motion of their horses, and not gripping the saddle with their knees at all;—the saddles, in fact, not possessing knee-pads. Probably no finer riders than these stockmen are to be found anywhere. A wild Western bull is an ugly customer to deal with, but the herdsmen have no fear, and quickly succeed in bringing the most intractable brute to terms. The men employed in the slaughter-houses are the most noted roughs, or, as the Chicago people say, "the hardest characters," in the city; and no respectable person goes near the Stock Yards after dark if he can help it.

On Sunday we walked outwards along Dearborn Avenue to Lincoln Park, which is nicely laid out, and being smaller than most American city parks, looks more like one of our own. Sunday is the day when the citizens turn out in their sleighs, and show themselves to an admiring public; and crowds were skating on the lake in the park, and generally making merry. The theatres are open on Sunday evening, and the day seems little observed. One reason of this no doubt is, that the people work too closely during the week, and take no holiday; many of the warehouses being opened at seven in the morning, and not closed until seven at night. And employers as well as employed go down to business at this early hour, remaining till the very close; accordingly, a great part of the city population take their recreation on Sunday. In the evening, however, we came upon an exactly opposite phase of things; for, on going to an Episcopal Church, we heard a sermon rather of the "revival" order. The clergyman appeared like any business man, being dressed in a surtout, with a coloured necktie. He preached with considerable force, and was evidently much in earnest; intimating prayer meetings for every night throughout the week. It was very strange to see how extremes met in the same city.

Next day I encountered Mr Smithson again in the hotel. He greeted me like an old acquaintance, and opened out at once. That man seemed always "spoiling" for a conversation.

"Glad to see you again, sir! Guessed you'd have left by now. And how is the prospect of business looking?"

"I told you I wasn't here on business."

"Of course! *I* understand quite well. You Britishers won't talk about a thing; but you are *on* it all the same, *I* know. Well, and have you been going around?"

"Yes, I have seen a good deal. And I had a nice ten-mile walk yesterday."

"A ten mile walk! The benignant Pharaoh! You are the maddest people, you English, that ever I knew! Why in thunder don't you take the cars?"

"I like walking for exercise; it does me good."

"Well now, I never! And such a waste of time, too!"

"You see, Mr Smithson, you and I look at it differently. I have no doubt you would rather walk a mile out of the way to find a car to take you half a mile; now, I like the walk itself."

"Is that really so? Well, and are you pleased with Chicago?"

"Chicago is undoubtedly a wonderful place. Take it all round, I never saw such business activity in my life."

"I guessed you'd say so. Take my word for it, sir, there's no better place for a man that really means going ahead; he is bound to succeed in Chicago. And it's a good city for a young man: we don't keep a young man down here just because he is young,—if he has the grit he is sure to rise."

"Still, a good many men with no lack of energy fail to get on. Energy doesn't always do it."

"If a man tries one line and don't succeed, he has just got to look around and try something else. Failure at first oughtn't to scare a man. He has only to start afresh, and he is certain to strike his luck at last. Do you see that gentleman sitting by the window?"

"The stout man with the red nose?"

"Yes, sir. Now, I know that man intimately: that man started fifteen years ago as a porter on State Street; then he drove a team; then he was warehouse clerk and railway superintendent. Then the railway got into difficulties; so he went into provisions, and got busted; struck out West, and was farmer and deputy-sheriff; busted again; came back to the city, and tried English cloths; busted once more;

took up ironmongery,—and now he is doing a boss trade in ironmongery and agricultural implements."

"We'd be inclined to call him a Jack of all trades, I fear!"

"Call him what you like, sir; you don't hurt *him*. He has hit the article, sir, and he is successful. Take my word for it, if you fail in one business, you don't need to be down-hearted; just start out lively and look around, and take the first opening that comes handy; work your level hardest, and you'll strike your luck at last. You may laugh at a man shifting his trade if you want to; but he succeeds in the end. That's what we look to."

"But most men have a special fitness for one business more than another."

"That's a mistake. A man can do anything, if he's fairly on it. English mechanics, now, that come out here, are often no good. If they don't find a job in their own trade right away, they loaf and get to drinking; and go from bad to worse. Then they curse the country. Now, an artisan coming to the States must set to cheerful and lump on the quay, or drive a car, till he finds something to suit. Once he begins loafing, he's done for. Loafers get no respect here. We don't care what a man does, so he does something, and it's honest. The man that works will rise, sir; the man that loafs can't."

"You certainly seem to have very few idlers in Chicago."

"They can't live here; there's no room for them. If we had been loafers, we'd not have been what we are now. Six years ago the business part of this city, four miles in length, was burnt to the ground; to-day it's built up again as secure and handsome as any European city. Business, sir, is increasing with simply gigantic strides. That's not the effect of loafers, you be certain!"

"But you have not the excessive experience of bad trade here that we have at home. If you were to have a stagnation such as we are now suffering, many of your population would be thrown out of work, and compelled to remain idle."

"Not at all; no man need remain idle in the States. If he can't get work in the city, he has only to strike out West. And that's exactly what he does; —he starts West right away, and takes land. There's plenty of room there."

"You have in that vast Western country a paradise for the unemployed such as no European nation possesses."

"Well, I guess we have. But we are main glad to see emigrants from Europe too. There's room for all."

Mr Smithson was right. Idle men do not thrive

in America. It is less of reproach to a man in the States to be a blackguard than a loafer. There is no scarcity of blackguards and desperate characters; but these all command a certain respect from the remarkable push with which they conduct their business. A disposition of extreme enterprise, and an ever cheerful alacrity with the pistol, completely remove from them the stigma of inactivity. You rarely see a broken-down man in America. If a man gets "busted" in any business, he either goes into it again at once, or else plunges into a new line without fear or hesitation. Two of the most prominent features of the American's character are his energy and adaptability. His adaptability is amazing; and is greatly born of self-confidence. He does not see why another man should be able to do anything which he himself could not do; and he will accordingly turn from book-keeping or newspaper editing to agriculture or housebuilding, with the most implicit belief in his own capability. And when this striking quality is backed by an indomitable energy, it ceases to appear strange why the American succeeds. (From the energy and singular disregard of conventionality which characterise Brother Jonathan, America has been aptly designated "Young John Bull working in his shirt-sleeves!")

CHAPTER XI.

A PRAIRIE VILLAGE.

IT was a village; but we would not have ventured so to describe it to the dwellers therein. To them it was a city; for had it not a main street, an embryo avenue, a railroad depôt, two hotels, and three churches? Its population numbered five hundred enlightened American citizens, and it stood emblazoned on the page of fame as Piper City. It owed this appellation to a being of the shadowy past, who shone through a traditional halo of semi-luminous obscurity by the cognomen of Piper, and who appears by the initiation of a store to have sown the first germ of the locality's present commercial magnitude. This information we gathered from sundry allusions thrown out by the inhabitants during our sojourn beneath the spreading wings of their civic polity.

Piper City is situated on the great Western prairie, some ninety miles to the south-west of Chicago. A Scotch friend of ours, occupying the post of banker there, being solicitous lest we should leave the States without seeing something of the more primitive side of Western life, invited us to spend a few days under his roof. So we left Chicago one fine frosty morning, sped—in a very slow train—over the flat snowy country, and duly reached our friend's abode in time for a warm dinner, and a warmer welcome. "We can't give you the splendour of the Palmer House," he said; "but we'll make you as comfortable as we can." Nor did he belie his word.

Our acquaintance with the manners and customs of the place began in an afternoon's quail-shooting. C——, the banker, being unable himself to leave his office, introduced us to a citizen named Nat Williams, who, he said, would take care to show us all that was to be seen. On the prairie, the citizens of a place are known as "the boys;" and Nat Williams was a "boy" of forty-five or thereby, whose earthly calling lay between digging wells and hunting,—the latter in its wide sense as embracing all sport, and more especially shooting and trapping. Nat was a fine fellow, and a thoroughly good companion, with a sunburnt face and a very dilapidated suit of clothes. He produced a sleigh, a pair of horses, and a gun; we likewise armed ourselves with guns, and the party set off, Nat predicting that we should have "a high old time." The sleigh, like most similar Western vehicles, was home-made, being simply an unpainted wooden box on runners, with two seats placed across.

It seemed strange to have a pair of horses for such an equipage; but no one on the prairie would think of driving a single animal. Though the load be light as a feather, a pair is always used. And the pair is designated a "span" or "team." Generally the team are horses, less frequently mules, and on occasion a horse and a mule.

Sleighing on the prairie is lively and exhilarating. The snow is crisp, and sparkles in the sun by its minute crystallisation; the air is brisk and keen; the sky is blue, without a cloud; and you wrap yourself in the rugs and spin along, feeling as bright and joyous as a lark. Our way lay along a narrow road, with snow-drifts banked up on either side against the close thorn hedges.

"How far is it to the shooting ground?" we asked Nat, as we bowled along.

"The shootin' ground? Calc'late we're on it now, as much as we're like to be. You jest keep your eyes skinned, an' look out for the trail of the birds in the snow—then we'll git out an' follow 'em up."

"But what will you do with the sleigh when we get out?"

"Why, jest let t' old thing rip till we git in again, o' course!"

"Then you'll have to tie up the horses?"

"Nary a bit. We'll run the sleigh into a drift,

and I guess the beasts won't quit till we come back. They won't need no hitchin!"

"Well, I'm blowed!" says Davis.

"Birds!" sings out Nat presently, turning the trap short into a four feet snow bank, and nearly capsizing us. "Get your guns now, and come along lively."

We tumbled out, and followed the footprints of the quail for a couple of hundred yards up the hedge, Nat leading warily.

"Thar!" says Nat, pointing with his finger, "see him?"

"Quail? Where?"

"Right afore you, to be sure, crouchin' a'neath the hedge. Whar's yer eyes? Get forrard now, quiet, an' fix him."

We saw a small bird, apparently a little bigger than a thrush, cowering under the hedge, and looking very solitary and miserable; accordingly we began to move up with deadly intent, Nat generously remaining behind, to give us the shot.

"Stop thar!" cries Nat, as we continue to approach. "Sure you're nigh enough now. Give it him now, give it him!"

"You wouldn't fire at him sitting, would you?"

"Sittin'! Why on 'arth not? O' course I would. I'd shoot him lyin'. Give it him, I tell ye!"

The bird remained sublimely indifferent during this colloquy. We moved on, hearing Nat mutter something about " British notions " and " dod-rotted folly." Presently, when we had advanced within ten yards, up got the quail.

Bang! bang! bang! bang!—four barrels. The bird flew leisurely away. Davis and I gazed at each other.

" Extraordinary! Swear I covered him."

" So did I, I know. Gun must have scattered."

Voice from behind, derisively—

" Calc'late you didn't strike him, any ways! Guess you'd best ha' done as I told you."

" Nat," says Davis majestically, " we never fire at a sitting bird. It would be cold-blooded murder."

" P'raps you might ha' nailed him if you had, all the same!"

We resumed the sleigh, extricated the horses from the snow-drift, and drove on; Davis remarking thoughtfully—" I can't understand how that bird escaped!"

" Wall," says Nat chuckling, " I calc'late I do. It was 'cos you didn't strike him!"

" But do you mean to say you always blaze at the birds sitting?"

"If I find 'em sittin', I do for sartin'. I want the bird, an' it don't differ a cent whether he's sittin' or flyin'. If he's sittin',—why, nat'rally, so much the better!"

We drove hither and thither, up and down the long straight lanes, looking for birds, and getting out every now and then to walk through the corn stubble in the fields. Prairie stubble is rather different from that over which Englishmen love to walk in September. The Indian corn is merely husked by the machines, and the stalks are left standing; so that cattle put in afterwards to graze present a peculiar appearance, the "stubble" being three or four feet above their backs! We did not carry home a large bag, but were happily enabled to convince Nat that we could (occasionally at least) bring down a quail flying.

In the early part of the winter there are a great many quail and prairie-hen about the fields, and they are killed in great numbers, there being no limitation as to trespass. The "hunter" can roam over any man's corn-fields as he lists. In spring and autumn wild ducks and geese appear in the swampy patches in countless flocks, literally darkening the sky when they take wing. In those seasons every male inhabitant goes out to shoot: and some very antique and decidedly unsafe pieces of artillery, dating perhaps from the War of Independence, are brought to light.

Customs in Piper City are delightfully primitive. There are three heavy meals in the day—breakfast at seven, dinner at noon, and supper at five. (Hot suppers at a late hour are an evil unknown.) The servants of the house—no longer servants, but "helps"—consider themselves on perfect equality with those whose wages they take, and sit at table with the family—although possibly rising to hand round dishes, if the inspiration strikes them :—which, however, it rarely does. Outdoor servants, such as field hands, are no exception to the rule, but gather round the social board with happy freedom. Generally the family dine in the kitchen.

In the West we really see the principle of social equality carried to its fullest extent. And no man need go to the West with a view to settle, unless he is prepared to accept the existing state of things; he will find himself powerless to make any change; he must conform to the ways of the place, or it will become too unpleasant to hold him. Improvement in social customs will come naturally with time; but no one man can hope to accelerate it. He who refuses to sit at table with his servants, will find it impossible to get servants; and a man must be ready to receive and welcome any neighbour who chooses to call and see him, otherwise he will be cut by the whole community. But if such visits be sometimes unseasonable, they are nearly always kindly meant; and provided the man receives them in the spirit in which they are intended, he will find his neighbours ever ready to help and like him. Dwellers on the prairie are kindly folks to each other, and always prepared to assist a neighbour in misfortune. So he who comes to settle must keep all old-world notions to himself, accept the state of society he finds, and make the best of it. Nor is that best so very bad. These rough Western settlers are a very different order of men from the lower classes of a European city. They are not stupid and sottish; they are not lazy like that model grievance, the British working-man; nor are they, like him, given to discontent and trades' unions. The British working-man of the eight hours' work and trades' union stamp would be sadly out of his element in the West. The Western settler is a man who thrives,—and he thrives by hard work. He means work, and does work, never thinking of long hours. The idler cannot live on the prairie; he is speedily despised and shunned, and soon disappears towards the slums of the city, where he sinks into whisky and oblivion.

But the settler is not to be judged by the hasty observer. For he is a strange anomaly, this Western man, and needs to be known to be understood. If a Cockney Crœsus, who had made his money in cheese, and was consequently disposed to regard himself as on a pinnacle of rank attained only by a select few of his own kind, were to spend two days in a prairie village, his account of the men he had met would probably be as follows:—

"Men—aw—of a class really unspeakable. Coarse people—aw;—too horridly rude and vulgar; clothed in rags—aw,—and covered with dirt and degradation. A depraved set—aw,—of an order really too dreadfully low. And—aw—incredibly uppish and impudent—aw,—with absolutely no idea of their own station. Men—aw—who actually stare you in the face, and—aw, aw—have actually no idea of whom they are talking to! Men—aw—who entirely forget their position—aw,—and are—aw—so debased that they—aw, aw—have the confounded impertinence not to take off their hats to a gentleman! Horrible!—aw,—altogether too horrible!"

But the stranger of ordinary sense will not thus mistake. There are reasons for everything. It is true that the settler's clothes are bad—perfectly true: they are worse than bad—they are often villainous. They show scant vestige of the original colour, and are ventilated by holes at all points. But the settler's labour in the fields is rough beyond what most persons know; all are alike engaged in it; there is no outsider to see them; and they do not care to spoil good garments. They are intelligent, these prairie men, and thoroughly acquainted with their business; possessing, moreover, a much larger information on general subjects than does the British labourer. As to independence of manner,—they have been born to a social state into which rank and class never entered, and so cannot be expected to admire or look up to that which they do not comprehend. And their innate consciousness of capability for their own vocation, arising from success in it, inspires them with a marked self-respect and self-reliance. They care not for king or kaiser, simply because they have never known them; and if a peer of England came among them, they naturally could not take in his position. If he tried to impress them with social superiority, they would merely laugh at him; in fact, in so far as he could not work with his hands and earn his own bread as they do, they would probably consider themselves superior to him.

The settler's spirit of equality and independence springs not from discontent at a felt supremacy of class, as in the case of the turbulent British working man,—but solely from his having failed to grasp the idea that there could be—under the sun—any class who might claim deference and dependence from him. Much of this idea of universal equality must fade away with an advancing refinement; but such of it as at present obtains, ceases to be obnoxious, when we regard its peculiar character. It is not on the prairie that the outcry is raised against an "effete and bloated British aristocracy;" the Western men are too simple and careless to trouble their brains about such a thing; that vapouring and offensive demonstration springs amid the cities, from hot-headed demagogues and newspaper men, whose misfortune is that knowing something, they have there stopped short, and know too little. But to the stranger, the Western settler is doubtless an unintelligible and unknown quantity at first. He sees a rough man, whose garb might qualify him to be the prince of mendicants,—he sees in that man's face a sturdy independence and self-respect,—then he is told that the man is worth three or four thousand dollars; and he takes some time to understand and reconcile the novel features.

A year's residence on the Illinois prairie would be particularly beneficial to some of our own countrymen, who incline to set too high a figure on their own importance; as they might there find for the first time a set of people who would not take them at their own valuation. They would return much wiser, if somewhat sadder men.

We used to gather in the evenings round C——'s

hospitable stove, to discuss the events of the day and the manners of Piper City. Seated one night in this way, Davis remarked, in a meditative tone,—

" Piper City seems to be just a reproduction of Chicago on a smaller scale."

" In what way ? " asked C——,

" It seems to be the outlet of produce for the country round about, and the centre of distribution for supplies."

" True, it is a good enough parallel. The farmers bring in their corn and hogs to be transported eastwards by rail, and buy at the stores all they want. You would notice that a Piper City store is rather a miscellaneous establishment ? "

" Rather ! I should just say it is ! "

" The farmer can get anything there, from pins and needles and tea and sugar, up to ploughs and reaping machines."

" There's no lack of activity in the place either ;— Piper city must do a good little business of its own."

" Well, I can give you in a moment the rough statistics of our yearly trade." And he rapidly pencilled down the following :—

ANNUAL EXPORTS.

Corn	$250,000
Hogs	60,000
Flax	50,000
Oats and Rye	10,000
	$370,000

ANNUAL IMPORTS.

As shown by gross amount of retail sales	200,000
Difference or profit	$170,000

"That's a handsome surplus for you to put into your pockets," said Davis, on glancing over the figures.

"Very fair; but it doesn't remain in our pockets long. That surplus goes out chiefly to the Eastern States, to pay investors their interest on farm mortgages."

"Indeed?"

"Yes; and one of the main branches of my business has to do with that. You see when the farmer wants to raise a mortgage loan upon his land, he comes to the bank, and we get the thing effected for him, acting as brokers. There is hardly a farmer about who has not a loan on his land."

"What does he need the money for? Is it to buy more land?"

"No, he has enough to do as a rule with his hundred acre lot. But he needs money for improvements, in the shape of increased hired labour, or farm buildings, or agricultural machinery."

"Ah! And does he get the loan readily?"

"If he is known to be ordinarily hardworking and sensible, people are glad enough to invest. The investor gets a first mortgage, and interest at eight or ten per cent."

"Rather high interest to be safe, isn't it?"

"Nothing can be safer. Suppose a man has a farm worth 3000 dollars, and wants to raise a 500 dollars loan, he gives you a first mortgage. If he doesn't pay up his interest when it is due, you foreclose. You couldn't wish anything safer than that? It is considered about the best secured investment that can be made."

"Very good—if only the investor, who may be a thousand miles from the spot, can rest assured that the land is honestly valued, and everything done on the square."

"There is small fear of false dealing; the land is valued by competent persons, and the mortgages are very carefully and conscientiously adjusted. It wouldn't pay to cheat, it would just be killing the goose with the golden eggs. I don't speak for Piper city only, but for the many similar places round. There are hundreds of little towns like this throughout the West, each with its banker and loan agent. There is a place like this every eight miles or so in the surrounding district."

"Why, there must be no end to them!"

"You must have noticed that in this country things are managed with great regularity and system. The mode of division and sub-division of land is admirable. The State is divided into counties, the counties are divided into townships, these into sections, those again into quarter sections, and even lower. Each of those divisions is a square. The townships are squares measuring eight miles each way, the sections a mile each way, and so on. And this regular arrangement of land makes the definition of any specific property in a deed of sale or transfer, a very easy and distinct matter,—much more so than in Britain, where one man's land runs into another's in all sorts of angles and corners."

"So it naturally will. Then each township has, I suppose, its town or city like this?"

"Exactly. And the town is generally placed upon the railway, so that it becomes the radiating centre of its eight mile district."

" That minute subdivision goes to prove that those little towns will never increase beyond a certain point. When the land within their radius is all fully cultivated, and producing to its highest extent, their development will there and then stop short. The land at its best can only produce up to a certain limit, and only support a certain number of persons; so when that limit is reached, the place will have attained its highest degree of prosperity."

" Undoubtedly, unless in years to come manufactures spring up, and give the place an artificial prosperity."

" People here are very primitive and unsophisticated, but I suppose they have learned the great lesson of how to get round one another in business?"

" Well, they are keen enough certainly, and know precious well what they are about; but they are very honest. Do you know we have hardly any crime here?"

" Indeed? Then you are peculiarly happy!"

" For one thing, we are rabid Good Templars. There has been a great deal of agitation about the liquor question in the State of Illinois; and each county is now allowed to decide for itself whether liquor is to be sold within its own bounds or not. Ford County, in which we are, has decided against liquor; so any man who wants a drink must have it bought outside of the county and sent to his own house. The people go pretty far too; for they look suspiciously even on the man who likes his glass of beer at dinner,—so much so that many a man doesn't drink, simply in case it might injure his business with his Good Templar neighbours."

"Rather hard luck for an English settler who holds to his native beverage!"

"Well, it may be extreme; but it unquestionably decreases crime and trouble. Then again, they're nearly all revivalists and strong Methodists in this district; and they stick to their religion. They hold regular meetings, and always pass round the hat most conscientiously."

"I should say they would seldom forget to do that."

"Yes, but it's often the literal process,—the preacher sends round his own hat. He doesn't invariably get much, however. There was a goodish thing in a place near this lately;—the minister held forth vigorously for upwards of an hour, and exhorted the people to give liberally; then he sent his hat on its travels. The castor went round the whole meeting, and came back without a solitary cent inside. The preacher looked eagerly into it, and seemed very downcast for a little; then he faced the assembly and exclaimed devoutly—'Anywise, it's a matter of supreme thankfulness that I've got my hat safe back from this congregation!'"

"He had them there neatly, I imagine!"

"Most completely."

"What about the lawlessness which we hear so much of at home as prevailing in the West? That would seem to be all rubbish."

"So it is, as regards settlers and decent citizens. Down in Texas and Kentucky they sometimes work with the pistol and bowie, but not in the West here;—at least, not unless you go very far West. The only people we have to fear hereabouts are tramps and professional thieves. But there are a good many of them,—desperate villains too. They work in gangs, and go ranging through the country. Their plan is usually to drop into a village like this on a night train, rob the bank or the most promising dwelling-house, and then get clear away by train again in a couple of hours."

"They must do the thing very quietly, or they'd be found out and nailed at the station."

"Sometimes they do work secretly, and sometimes with the greatest effrontery. They may clean out a private house very quietly; but when they mean to rifle the bank it's not quite so pleasant. They know that in the bank all the money is locked in the safe, and they can't hope to force the safe in less than two or three hours' time; so they enter the banker's dwelling-house, pull him out of bed with a revolver to his head, and force him to come over to the bank with them and open his own safe. That's called 'bull-dosing' a man."

"Uncommonly nice for the banker! But is there no chance of his resisting?"

"Well, we prairie bankers generally sleep with our pistols ready to hand; but that's little use if you are waked up to find a blackguard at your face with a bead on you already from his own weapon. It's a case of turning out or being coolly murdered."

"Have you ever been served in this fashion?"

"Never myself, I am thankful to say; though some of my neighbours have. But there is a recent invention which completely upsets the burglars."

"What is that?"

"The time-lock safe. This safe has a pair of chronometers inside, connected with the lock. These are wound up daily, and are so constructed that at a certain hour in the evening a bar falls and shoots a bolt, and at a corresponding hour in the morning the bar is raised and the bolt withdrawn. In this way the safe is locked every night *on the inside*, and can't be opened even by the owner. So it's no use 'bull-dosing' a man, if he can't possibly open his safe till the fixed time in the morning."

"That would be a splendid contrivance, certainly, if the burglar could only be brought to regard it in the light of reason; but he would most likely shoot you out of pure rage at being thwarted, when you told him you had a time-lock."

"The time-lock prevents the burglary being ever attempted,—that's the special beauty of it. Every time-lock safe that is sold is advertised by the sellers; and all burglars who aspire to safe-robberies are very careful to find out beforehand what kind of safe they have to assail; so if they know a man to have a time-lock, they give up their idea without more ado."

"I should fancy, then, that every Western banker would have a time-lock?"

"So he has, if he can afford it. The chronometer lock costs £100 extra, which is no small consideration. But the sense of security is worth the money."

"What is the object of having two chronometers?"

"In case one should stop or go wrong. If one were to stop during the night, the other would still draw back the bolt at the proper time in the morning. It would never do if the chronometer were to get out of order and keep the safe shut, for to break open such a safe would be simply to ruin it for the future. So the two chronometers provide against all contingencies."

"Yankee invention has outstripped us there!"

"From the fact that Yankee necessity is greater. Property in the West is not efficiently protected by police as at home, so extraordinary means have to be resorted to for its security."

"I see that American safes are worked chiefly by alphabetic locks, a key-word or a formula of letters being used instead of a key."

"Yes; and that too is far ahead of the British plan. The lock is as good as a Milner, and the key is much safer in your brain than in your pocket. And now, as the hour is late, I think we'll go to bed."

In driving over the prairie, there is no scenery of any kind. Fields of corn stalks six or seven feet high stretch away on every side for hundreds of miles, without the slightest suggestion of a hill. Occasionally there is a small grove of young maple trees, but no tree of any size. Now and then you come upon some almost stagnant ditch or creek, but never a pond or sheet of water. The water for house use comes from a depth of seventy feet or so, and is pumped up into wells at the surface by small windmills. It is curious for the first time to see a number of private houses each with a windmill in the garden; and you begin to marvel less at the huge exports of American flour,—till you are told that the mills are only for water-raising. Well-boring is quite a trade on the prairie; and this kind of well is spoken of as an " Artesian " well.

The prairie roads are as straight as a blameless life, intersecting each other every mile or so at strict right angles. They are bordered by prickly hedges of osage orange, very like hawthorn on a larger scale, and bearing a species of orange in the autumn. It is a very painful experience to penetrate an osage hedge, and one which will indelibly impress itself upon the sufferer's memory.

The weather was very cold all the time of our stay in Piper City, averaging ten degrees below zero; and the want of shelter from the searching wind on the boundless flat doubled its intensity. We could not keep water in our room at night, as it would have been frozen solid by morning. (The prairie settler is not always very conscientious in his ablutions during the winter, finding a layer of natural dirt very admirable as a substitute for additional underclothing.) Awaking in the morning, we used to find our breath issuing from between moustache and beard stiff with ice; while the fantastic fretwork of Jack Frost upon the window panes would have driven a pattern designer wild. Davis' pipe cracked in his pocket, the moisture inside freezing and splitting the wood. The good folks of the prairie wear very thick clothing in the winter season, muffling up ears and hands with special care. All the men have high boots, with their trousers tucked inside; and long india-rubber boots are often used for the snow, the latter being in Western *parlance* designated "gum-boots."

The houses of a prairie village are all of wood, painted white; and the appearance of the settlement is that of a cluster of low white cottages, with a church spire rising in their midst. The church is no exception to the rule, being also of wood. The houses are roofed with wooden shingles, of the same shape and size as slates; and looking very like slates by being painted black. Shingles are cheaper, and fully as suitable as slates, the latter being apt to crack and split from the intense frost.

The houses of the better class are lined with felt, to exclude the cold in winter and the heat in summer; the latter, we were told, being as excessive in its season as is the frost. Summer comes with a rush on the close of winter, there being hardly any spring: in April the sun begins to blaze fiercely, the snows melt, there is a period of universal and inextricable mud, and then vegetation bursts with a leap into full meridian. The corn-fields shoot forth into lusty verdant life, and the snow-drifts by the roadside are replaced by glowing beds of brilliant flowers. In the dog-days mosquitoes and snakes abound; the former a torture beyond expression, the latter for the most part harmless. On the unturned prairie there are a number of rattlesnakes, but these speedily disappear as the land becomes broken to cultivation. Prairie folks say that they have little dread of a rattlesnake's bite, if they can only get plenty of raw whisky within half-an-hour of being bitten. They drink the whisky straight on till intoxication appears; and whenever they are drunk, they are cured. The whisky keeps up the circulation, which the snake poison would cause to cease; and so powerful is the poison, that two or three quarts of whisky are required to make an adult man drunk after having been bitten. A little girl has been said in such a case to drink a quart straight off before becoming intoxicated; and I am told that even the Good Templars do not refuse to adopt this remedy.

The majority of the settlers claim American parentage; but a considerable proportion are of Dutch, German, and Scotch extraction, not a few Dutch and German names being noticeable. Almost every nationality is represented on the prairie, in the ancestors at least of the present inhabitants; but most of the denizens have been born where they live, and are "Western men," pure and simple. After once meeting the genuine, unadulterated article, there is little fear of your failing to recognise him on any future occasion.

Farming in Illinois is a strong, healthy life ; and if a man enters upon it without any high-flown notions, he is likely to do well in it, and be happy. It is decidedly rough at first, there is little society, and the scenery is painfully monotonous ; but if he can put up with those drawbacks, and work hard, he is nearly certain to prosper. An improved farm can be purchased for thirty dollars, or six pounds, an acre.

So we left Piper City after some days, having seen and experienced a phase of American life which not every tourist has the opportunity of doing ; and having learned with no common interest something of manners on the Western prairie.

CHAPTER XII.

DETROIT AND NIAGARA.

HAVING now penetrated as far towards "the home of the setting sun" as occasion permitted, we turned about our faces, and proceeded eastwards to Detroit and Niagara. From Chicago to Detroit is a distance of two hundred and eighty-four miles; which the trains of the Michigan Central Railroad accomplish in ten hours. Unfortunately a thick snow-storm came on during our journey; and we were thus prevented from seeing more of the district through which we passed, than that it was low undulating country, tolerably well cleared. One of the peculiar amenities of American railway travelling is the inefficiency of the lighting apparatus in the carriages; and an application of mine to the Pullman attendant for fuller illumination was met in the following highly satisfactory way.

"Look here," I said, "can't you turn up those lamps a bit;—I want to read."

"Very sorry, sir, but they ain't lamps. They're candles, and I can't make them burn any brighter."

"Then why on earth don't you have lamps?"

(In a confidential whisper). "Well, you see, sir, when the cars are overturned, candles ain't no ways so dangerous as oil-lamps."

"What! Then you coolly calculate upon the cars being overturned, do you?"

"Well—um!"—and he smiled sweetly; and with a benign expression withdrew.

We were lucky enough, however, to escape overturning on this particular occasion, and reached Detroit in safety; where we took up our quarters at the Russell House. The first thing to impress us in this establishment was our bed-room bell. This necessary appurtenance, though possessing the outward characteristics of an ordinary electric bell, was yet dignified beyond others of its species by being labelled "Hotel Annunciator." We were naturally curious to become acquainted with the process of annunciation, but found it to eventuate simply in the appearance of a porter. Jonathan is immensely fond of high-sounding names. He would much rather have a word polysyllabic than appropriate. His hoist or lift is an "elevator," the check-strap of his omnibus is a "communicator," his telegraphic needle is an "indicator,"—and so on. The next prominent feature of the Russell House was the unexampled heat of the reading-room. To sit in this apartment in a perfectly quiescent state was possible, though at the expense of much discomfort; but to attempt to read or write was simply to bring the perspiration trickling from every pore, and brave imminent risk of suffocation. No Briton could long inhabit such a den, and we were soon driven out in a bodily condition akin to moist blotting-paper; but the American guests seemed actually to revel in the heat. Nothing—except, perhaps, eating—seems to afford the American the same lively degree of satisfaction as being slowly boiled alive. Rapid and promiscuous eating, and hot rooms, go far to account for sallow faces and disordered livers.

We met a very intelligent negro waiter in the Russell House, a pleasant-looking, grizzled man of fifty, who seemed to bear a strong affection for the British. After placing our dinner before us, he bent down to me with a broad smile irradiating a vision of gleaming ivory, and whispered—

"From the old country, sa?"

"Yes," I replied.

"'Fraid the old country in a bad state just now, sa."

"Ah! How do you make that out?"

"Well, sa, bad business times sa, and troubles with the other nations, sa. Think Russia is great enemy of the old country, sa. Guess Russia wants to make great war with you, sa."

"You think so, do you?"

"Yis, sa. Russia very deceitful nation, sa, and Gork—Gosh—Gortsk—"

"Gortschakoff?"

"Yis, sa. Gorshuffkoff big villain, sa. Wants to take India from you, sa. Very bad man, sa. It was fine thing your Duke Beaksfield bringing troops to Malta, sa."

"You admire Lord Beaconsfield then, I suppose?"

"Ah, yis, sa. Very great statesman, sa. 'Stror'-nary man, sa!"

"Why, my good friend, you are a regular politician! You ought to be in Congress."

"Me, sa? Ah, no! me poor man, sa."

"Where did you manage to pick up all your information?"

"I read the daily papers, sa. Get you some more squash, sa?" And off he trotted for the vegetable in question.

Returning in a minute, he proceeded—

"Can you tell me, sa, how they look on the black man in England, sa?"

"Oh! we are very favourable to the black man, but we haven't many black men at home."

"No, sa? Then England not a good place for the black man to go to, sa?"

"He will be well treated if he comes over; but we

have no room for him there. We have too many working men of our own already."

"Ah yis, sa! Then he best stop in the States, sa."

"I should say so. Besides, you wouldn't like our raw, damp climate, and our fogs. But are you not happy enough in America now? You have got freedom, and lots of advantages if you like to take them; and you have several coloured men in the Government of the country."

"Oh yis, sa. The black man very well off in the States now, sa. But I thought I'd like to ask 'bout England, sa."

"You don't object to the abolition of slavery, I imagine? Were you ever a slave?"

"Yis, sa. I was slave for thirty-two years, sa."

"And how did you like it? Were you kindly treated?"

"I had a very good place, sa. But some of us were very ill-used, sa. I was happier than the most, sa."

"However, I don't suppose you quarrel with abolition?"

"Ah no, sa! We have justice now, sa. More beef-steak, sa!—yis, sa." And away he went.

This man was a specimen of the negro considerably above the average; for good humour is decidedly more the characteristic feature of the black man than supernatural intelligence. The negro is very loquacious, if you only give him the opportunity; and if he possesses any information, he is particularly proud of airing it.

Detroit is a quiet, pleasant city, with nothing very remarkable about it. The streets are broad, but not thronged with earnest wayfarers like the Chicago thoroughfares. One snowy morning I was walking leisurely along, enveloped in a white mackintosh, when I was unexpectedly accosted by a passer-by—

"Didn't buy that india-rubber coat in the States, sir, I guess?"

"No," said I, in some surprise; "I got it in the old country."

"Thought so. Feel disposed to trade, sir?"

"Well, no," answered I, still more surprised, "I think I'd rather not part with it."

"If you feel like letting it go for four dollars, we'll make a dicker" (bargain).

"Why, my good sir, can't you buy one here for yourself?"

"Not a thin white one like that. Guess I've taken a fancy to yours."

"Well, I'm afraid we can't do business. I think, with your permission, I'll stick to my waterproof."

"All right, sir. Don't mind my mentioning it, I suppose? Good-day, sir."

And he passed on.

I subsequently noticed that a thin white waterproof like mine was a rarity in America; and more than once again was I solicited to "trade" my own. In the end, indeed, I came rather to regret not having accepted some one of those offers, as I had not occasion to use the garment more than half-a-dozen times in as many months. A rainy day was a most unusual occurrence.

The "lions" of Detroit are the City Hall, the Public Library, and the Penitentiary. The latter institution is the State prison of Michigan, to which offenders from all parts are consigned: and we were most politely shown all over it, finding it beautifully clean and well ordered, and really a most attractive home to intending criminals. The convicts live remarkably well; being usually allowed meat twice a day, and obtaining permission to chew tobacco—though not to smoke—as a reward for good conduct. Four-fifths of the crime is said to result from drink. Some very desperate characters were undergoing sentence at the time of our visit; one gentleman was pointed out (not without a tinge of pride), as having killed with his revolver forty-seven men, for whom he had as many nicks on the handle of his weapon when captured. This redoubtable blackguard was physically a poor specimen, small and weakly, and by no means the sort of hero whom a twopenny romance would depict as the probable author of so much bloodshed. He was imprisoned for four years only; the authorities having been able to convict him merely of common assault and robbery, though his misdeeds were notorious; consequently at the expiry of his term, he will be turned loose again upon the world, to do still more mischief. It is right, however, to state, that the revolting catalogue of murders indicated had been chiefly committed far out on the Western frontier, where it is extremely difficult to collect adequate legal proofs of a crime. But punishments in the States seem as a rule too lenient to be deterrent; which goes far to account for the lynch law we frequently hear of from the remoter districts. Peaceable citizens, fearing lest the criminal be dealt with too lightly for the public safety, take the law into their own hands, and make short work with the offender.

The American blackguard, of whom the interesting individual whom we saw in Detroit Penitentiary is a sample, is very handy with his pistol; but is said to be often a coward in so far as fair fighting with his hands is concerned. He does not object to be shot or stabbed, but entertains a mortal dread of a thrashing.

A short stay sufficed to exhaust the wonders

of Detroit: and we started for Niagara by the Great Western Railroad of Canada. Detroit stands upon the Detroit River, which is at that point the boundary line between the States and Canada; the small town of Windsor being opposite upon the Canadian side. The nearest way from Detroit to Niagara lies through Canada, parallel to the northern shore of Lake Erie; and immediately after leaving Detroit Station, we passed over the river to Windsor. The train was run on to a steamer, in which rails were fixed for the purpose, transported bodily across the stream, and run off on to the rails on the Canadian side. The boat, some three hundred feet long, and very broad, crunched through the floating masses of ice on the river as though they had been matchwood. The train proceeded at a nice jog-trot, and we pursued our way with a certain "homelike" feeling at being once more beneath the British flag. As we advanced into Canada, the appearance of the people changed considerably. Beards and whiskers began to decorate fresh, rosy faces; while in the States men either shave closely, or grow only the moustache; and the farther we went, the stronger and more healthy did the people look. They seemed of a very Scotch type—some being even as "Hielan' looking" as the veritable "Phairshon." Reaching the town of Hamilton, we were thrilled by a vision of stalwart fellows in great Kilmarnock bonnets, returning from curling, with their brooms and curling stones. On remarking to a fellow passenger that the Canadian looked a different style of man from the Yankee, he laughed, and said, "Yes, we Canadians know how to live. We take plenty of exercise, and don't ruin our constitutions by improper living. When we are hungry, we go for a good cut of roast beef and a pot of ale." And the speaker was in his own person a remarkably good exponent of his assertion.

As we passed beside the Bay of Hamilton—a large inlet from Lake Ontario, our attention was drawn to a number of small black huts far out on the ice; and on inquiring what they were, we were told that they belonged to fishermen, who thus sheltered themselves from the wind and snow, while they pursued their calling through holes cut in the ice.

We proposed taking up our abode at the village of Suspension Bridge, on the American bank of the Niagara River, a mile and a half below the Falls; and just before reaching the station, we passed over the Suspension Bridge itself. The bridge serves a double purpose, having the railway line above, and a covered roadway beneath. The train moved across very slowly; and we heard—indeed, almost felt—every plank of the structure straining and cracking with the keen frost. Looking down on the great river from the platform of the car, we failed to be impressed with fitting wonder and awe; for in the dim evening light the stream seemed little bigger than a large Highland river in flood. But this was only the effect of the darkness. It calls up, however, an amusing anecdote. A friend of ours once visited the Falls in company with an old Scotch farmer and a large party of strangers; when to his horror the old gentleman exclaimed, so loudly as to be heard by all,—" Hout mon, they're jist naething ava' tae the Fa's o' Clyde !" Of course the rest of the party were simply convulsed; and our friend himself was very soon forced to join in the general merriment.

Arrived at Suspension Bridge, we established ourselves in a rambling wooden hotel, where we were boarded and lodged for the moderate sum of two dollars per day. The living was good and the beds were clean; but a truly Stoic simplicity was apparent about the furniture and walls—highly refreshing after the palatial splendour of the Palmer House, Chicago, and such establishments. The railway station was barely thirty yards from the hotel; so that we had the privilege of studying the different variations of the railway whistle, which was in a decidedly major key, and recurred with gratifying regularity every few minutes. The public sitting-room, some twenty feet by ten, was almost filled by a gigantic stove; so that we were driven to sit in our bedroom,—in which the only modern article of furniture was the spittoon. The chest of drawers and looking-glass appeared to be coëval with the Declaration of Independence; while the towel-rail was entirely pre-historic. From the peculiar construction of the latter, caution had to be used in approaching it, the bars being much given to swinging sharply round and striking the unwary on the eye.

There are two drawbacks to Niagara Falls—guides and gratuities. Every other man you meet is, or professes to be, a guide. His plan of action is as follows. Assaulting the stranger vigorously, he pledges himself to conduct him to all the points of interest for, let us say, a dollar. The stranger, deeming this to be advantageous and reasonable, closes with the offer; and a simultaneous smile of evil satisfaction—denoting intense obliquity of moral purpose—is seen to overspread the guide's countenance. The latter forthwith suggests a sleigh, as more agreeable than procedure on foot; the unsuspecting victim complies. The guide immediately signals an accomplice in the person of a sleigh-driver, who has been hovering in the vicinity; the party get in, and drive off. (The hire of the sleigh is from two to three dollars.) They visit first, we will say, the Whirlpool Rapids (admission fifty cents); turn back, and proceed upwards to the American Fall; then across the Upper Suspension Bridge (toll seventy-five cents). Arrived on the Canadian side, the stranger is borne to the Prospect House, overlooking the Horse Shoe Fall,—where the sleigh is temporarily put up. The guide has a perfect understanding with the proprietor of this hostelry, and delivers the victim into his hands for the time being. The proprietor pounces upon him, inserts him in a suit of oil-skins, and cripples his feet with ice spikes, to enable him to go down the rock and behind the Falls. For the privilege of risking his neck on the crazy ice-covered staircase, he is mulcted in a dollar. Emerging again into the upper world, and making his escape from the oil-skins, he is dragged within the hotel, and there obliged to purchase a variety of photographs and geological specimens; the latter bearing a curious family resemblance to road metal. (These interesting mementoes will amount, at the lowest figure, to two dollars.) Then the victim is relentlessly conducted to a camera obscura (twenty-five cents); and subsequently to a museum. Davis and I, having a wholesome horror of all museums, strenuously resisted, and just succeeded in evading the last infliction. At this juncture a photographer appears, and earnestly presses upon the visitor the desirability of being immortalised and handed down to posterity, as the prominent figure in a picture, of which the Falls constitute the background. We declined to recognise this appeal—basing our refusal on the plea that we did not wish to spoil the scenery; and the photographer, evidently unaccustomed to the introduction of such highly æsthetic grounds of argument, desisted from farther pressure. At last, having secured his pound of flesh, the Shylock of the Prospect House regretfully resigns the stranger again to the guide; who has been having a glass of beer and a cigar—doubtless on the footing of brokerage,—and who has the effrontery to gaze upon his unhappy victim with a face seemingly unconscious of villainy. Then back to the starting-point once more, —when the cicerone is likely to be impressed by the conviction that his services have been in requisition for a longer time than he contemplated when indicating one dollar as suitable remuneration; so the much-wronged stranger plunges again into his pocket, hands over two dollars, and bids his attendant begone, to return no more. And then he finds that his expenditure has been exactly nine dollars, or one pound sixteen.

At Niagara every bit of scenery has its money value. But the dollars ought not to be reckoned, for there is but one Niagara; and it is one of the singularly few places in America where this petty extortion exists. The American tourist coming to Britain, to a constant atmosphere of exorbitant hotels, high-priced ruins, and insatiable hirelings, has undoubted reason to complain; but not so the British traveller in America. The system of gratuities, or "tips," is still unknown in the States; or, if known, it is only in its infancy. In the latter case, it ought to be carefully strangled at the outset, or it will prove a most unthankful bantling.

The Niagara guide is not a bad fellow after all; and he is undoubtedly useful, being possessed of abundant information, practical and legendary, about the different places of interest. He conducts you to exactly the best view-points; he tells you that the water is wearing away the rock over which it precipitates itself at the rate of five inches in the year, so that the Falls are receding every twelve-month to that extent; he enumerates the persons who have been killed at the spot, with the precise manner of their decease; and he recounts the story of the "Maid of the Mist." The last is so exciting, that I am tempted to give it here.

From the foot of the Falls, for a mile down the river, the channel is wide and deep, and the water comparatively peaceful. But just below this calm space, the banks contract and the stream shallows, while the tremendous volume of water, thus confined and accelerated, rushes downwards between perpendicular ridges with awful velocity. This part of the river is called " The Rapids;" and it abounds in rocks, sharp bends, and foaming whirlpools or maelströms. So much to explain the situation. On the placid stretch close beneath the Falls, a little steamer named the " Maid of the Mist" was wont to ply, conveying sightseers backwards and forwards—now behind the spray curtain hanging over the foot of the cataract, and again down stream to the point where the waters begin to boil and eddy at the neck of the Rapids. She was a tiny cockle-shell, a mere steam launch, propelled by paddles. After some time, she was found by her owners to be a losing speculation; and notice was received that she was about to be arrested for debt. Then the captain, hearing of the proposed arrest, cast about in his mind how to save his ship. Once lying in the neutral waters of Lake Ontario, a dozen miles below, she would be beyond the power of the bailiffs: but to this haven of security there was only one path, and that lay through the fearful and hitherto untried torrent of the Rapids. But the captain's was a daring spirit; and he determined to run his little craft through, or go to pieces with her. The greatest terror of the undertaking lay in the fact that the extent of the danger was unknown. "What man has done, man can do;" but no man had ever before dreamt of shooting Niagara Rapids,—and the appearance of these was sufficient to appal the bravest. Here the torrent rises madly up seven or eight feet into a hollow recurving wave, evidently caused by some sunken rock reaching almost to the surface; there it sweeps fiercely round and round into a dark whirlpool, flattening towards the centre, and seemingly powerful enough to suck a larger body than the little "Maid" down into its gurgling depths. But the captain had taken his resolution, and was not to be daunted. One fine morning the "Maid of the Mist" was seen to get up steam, and leaving her moorings, to point down stream. No spectator imagined that she was not on her ordinary errand; nor supposed that on reaching her accustomed bourne at the top of the Rapids, she would do otherwise than turn round and come back again. But she seemed strangely daring that morning. The usual turning place was passed; and the little vessel began to shoot downwards faster and faster. Could anything be wrong? No; the captain was seen grasping the wheel, and standing composed as usual. She could only be trying a somewhat more venturesome trip;—she would turn presently. But still onward—faster and faster—till the onlookers grow pale. She cannot turn now, she is doomed to destruction: no power of engines or steam can stem the current backwards, so far has she gone. But the captain still stands cool and unmoved, the wheel in his hands, and his face fixed right ahead; the boat leaps forward under her fullest head of steam, and shoots headlong into the raging Rapids. The man is a raving suicide! Onward, onward, at a terrible speed—through beneath the Suspension Bridge;—rushing, dashing, bounding, into the thick of the turmoil. And the truth dawns upon the horror-stricken gazers. *He means taking her right through.* But he cannot do it; he will be lifted on one of those terrible waves, and shattered to atoms on the sunken rock. And he has the Whirlpool Rapids to pass;—no earthly thing can live there—he will be caught in the tumult and whirled round and round inwards to the vortex, and then down, down, down, to the bottom of the black abyss. But not yet,—still the "Maid" leaps furiously on. There, that huge hollow wave, with the crest of angry foam, and the daylight shining through its green mass, has caught her and thrown her upwards—then forwards with a crash. She is gone now. No, it is only the funnel broken short off, and the starboard paddle-box torn away. She is rushing down still, and the captain is still at his post, gripping the wheel with the tenacity of death. And now she is through the

Whirlpool—how, no man can tell—and forwards, forwards, forwards, mad and resistless. Five minutes more, and the danger is over: the broken water is behind, and the boat slides into the smooth broadening channel below; battered and exhausted, but victorious. She has accomplished what no boat has ever done, and what no boat will ever do again;—she has shot the Rapids of Niagara. And so down the now placid stream, till she floats on the bosom of Lake Ontario;—not the gay lively "Maid of the Mist" that left the Falls an hour ago,—but the " Maid of the Mist" still. And the captain and engineer, the two souls who compose her crew, moor her in the lake, safe from the bailiffs, and saved through a vastly more awful peril. Such is the tale of the "Maid of the Mist:" and if the heart of the listener thrills while he attends, what must have been the excitement which filled the actual spectators of the deed ! Instead of being preserved as a sight for after visitants, in the same shattered condition in which she completed her voyage, the "Maid of the Mist" has been repaired, and is now acting as a tow-boat on Lake Ontario.

Any description of Niagara Falls we shall not enter upon. They have been amply described by others—described and re-described, *usque ad nauseam;* for comparatively few delineations succeed in conveying any adequate idea of the reality. The world has been flooded with photographs—taken from one side, and taken from the other—from above, from below, from behind, from before—in summer and in winter. The Falls have been photographed in every conceivable aspect, locally and phenomenally; and a good photograph will go farther in the way of description than many words. This much we may say,—that the scene grows in grandeur the longer it is beheld. The British tourist gazes on Niagara with admiration and awe: the American "regrets that so much magnificent water-power should be wasted." But while thus deploring the unhappy loss of practical power, the American is very proud of his Falls; considering them "extremely rustic," and being particularly desirous that they should be seen and appreciated by strangers.

The Niagara River between the Falls and the Rapids was frozen hard during our visit, and great scenic attractions were held out as characterising the passage of the ice-bridge; so we duly made the crossing. The river bank is lofty and precipitous; and we were lowered to the foot through a covered way in a car running upon rails, and worked by a rope and hydraulic power. (Toll, of course, fifty cents). The descent looked rather unpleasant; but the rope was a great hawser of Manila hemp, capable, we were assured, of supporting eighty tons perpendicularly, while our car weighed only twelve hundredweight. Deposited at the bottom, we proceeded to cross the river on the ice-bridge; which was simply a narrow path cut through the blocks of ice, which lay jammed in irregular masses across the stream. Many of these blocks were ten feet high, and it would have been a very laborious task to scramble across without the aid of the path. On the very middle of the ice-bridge stood a rude hut, with a signboard, on which were inscribed the two announcements, "Centre House" and "Brandy Strate"* (*sic*); it being considered only natural that parties paying their tribute to the glories of Niagara should feel desirous of a "nip" in honour of the occasion. From the centre of the bridge, looking upwards to the two great Falls, the American and the Horse Shoe, the view was especially grand.

One of the finest sights at Niagara is the New Suspension Bridge just below the Falls. This structure, when seen in its span from a little distance along the bank, seems almost as beautiful a work of art as the Falls are a masterpiece of Nature. Painted white, and covered with snow, it looks as slender and airy as gossamer; and it is stayed up on both sides by countless white guys stretching down to the

* Brandy neat.

shore far below, which glisten in the brilliant sunlight like so many silver threads. This bridge is thirteen hundred feet in length, and is said to be the longest suspension bridge in the world; while its height above the stream is one hundred and ninety feet.

But the points of beauty and interest about Niagara are so many in number, and of such a character, that he who desires to become acquainted with them can do so only by visiting the place for himself.

CHAPTER XIII.

THE QUEEN CITY OF THE WEST.

THE Queen City of the West, as Canadians are sometimes pleased to designate Toronto, stands opposite to Niagara, forty miles across Lake Ontario. In summer, steamers make the passage in two or three hours; but the port of Toronto being ice-bound in winter time, we travelled by rail, doubling round the western end of the lake, a distance of some eighty miles. When crossing the Canadian frontier, the traveller is happily little troubled by the difference in moneys:—American and Canadian dollars are taken indiscriminately along the frontier and in places adjoining; and it is only when penetrating some distance into either country, that you need to be provided with its special currency. From a Customs Revenue point of view, the great extent of land frontier is a drawback, as offering peculiar facilities for smuggling; it being necessarily a more difficult task to keep watch over an extended line of country than over a seaboard. Up till the present year, American smugglers have been more ready to avail themselves of this opportunity than Canadian, the American import duties being so excessive; but now that a Conservative Government has raised the Dominion tariff, Canadian operators will not be less alive to the advantage of conveying into their country American manufactured goods free of impost.

Toronto is situated on the plain, on the north-western shore of the lake. It is a city of recent growth, dating its importance within the last fifty years; and having been till comparatively lately known as York,—formerly " Little York"—to distinguish it from its great neighbour at the mouth of the Hudson. For many years after the colonisation of Canada, people did not think of advancing westwards; being content to remain in the earlier cities of the eastern provinces. But as the cities of Montreal and Quebec, with their surrounding districts, became more thickly populated, enterprising men began to tend inwards, to seek in the fertile lands of the West that livelihood and prosperity which seemed yearly less easy of attainment near the seaboard. And the wonderful facilities of the great tract of Ontario as a producing country having been proved, a number of towns quickly sprang up, of which Toronto is the chief. We made a somewhat lengthened stay in the city, being the guests of friends, and owing much to Canadian hospitality, which in its heartiness and extent can be compared only with Highland or Irish.

As a city, Toronto is hardly striking. It is designed, of course, on the American plan of square blocks and long straight streets. The Toronto people affirm that Yonge Street is forty miles in length; but admit on further question that it finds its northern limit on the forest shores of Lake Simcoe. King Street is the Strand and Pall Mall of the place, where everybody drives, promenades, goes shopping, and gazes upon his (or her) neighbour. It was refreshing to us to see once more such names as "King Street," "Queen Street," and "Adelaide Street," after dwelling so long in a country which affects to scorn monarchy and its forms, and where the people have the woful insensibility to designate their city streets by numbers. Toronto has some fine public buildings and warehouses, chiefly of stone; and its more aristocratic streets are lined with pretty brick villas. It has a University, in appearance very similar to that of Glasgow, though on a smaller scale; (and like it, possessing a tower unfinished for want of funds). From the top of this tower, such as it was, we had a bird's eye view of the city. A transatlantic city, however, should not be seen from a height; as the number of small wooden houses, each in its own little plot of ground, which lie around the central portion, considerably detract from the dignity of the place. Passing along a street, you may remark a wooden house at intervals without being unfavourably impressed; but when you ascend to an eminence, and see a great number of such erections in one comprehensive glance, your artistic sense receives a severe shock.

Next to the University may be mentioned Knox College, for divinity students; where rising theologians are not only taught, but also "washed and boarded," for the surprisingly low figure of three dollars or twelve shillings per week. This sum does not of course pay expenses, but students are assisted to a certain extent from the funds of the institution. The only other noteworthy building is Osgood Hall, in which are the Law Courts and other rooms where lawyers assemble themselves together. The number of lawyers in Toronto is remarkable; and yet I am not given to understand that Western Canadians are more litigiously inclined than other men. Still there the lawyers are, and they are seen to thrive,—a starving lawyer, indeed, has never been met with in the world's history! There are three clubs, the Toronto, the National, and the United Empire; the first non-political, the second and third liberal and conservative respectively. And there is the Queen's Park, a handsome enclosure with pleasant carriage drives and tall trees; and the inevitable group of cannon taken at Sebastopol, (so distinctive of every truly British park.)

Toronto possesses a cathedral; and exhibits, indeed, an unusual fondness for churches;—this being carried so far, that one of the principal streets is named "Church Street," from the number of ecclesiastical edifices which line its extent. The churches are of every denomination—Episcopal, Presbyterian, Baptist, Methodist, Negro Methodist, and Roman Catholic. It is not every city which offers to its inhabitants such peculiar advantages.

The Parliament house of the Province of Ontario is situated in Toronto; and presents outwardly the appearance of a grain store. Each of the seven Canadian Provinces has a Provincial Assembly or Parliament, to transact its own affairs; while at Ottawa, the capital of the Dominion, there are two Houses, constituting the Dominion Parliament, which assumes the conduct of general Canadian politics. But the Provincial Parliament of Ontario is very much like a town-council. On our visit it wore a universal sleepy aspect, and an honourable member was dilating on the faults and failings of the City Gas Company, to an audience one-half of whom were asleep, and the other half conversing with each other on general subjects. There were several amusing urchins in the shape of messengers, clad in black jackets and knickerbockers, with white neckcloths, whose mission seemed to lie in fetching glasses of water to such legislators as were afflicted with thirst; —and who did not add to the dignity of the House, either by their dress or their behaviour; for when not engaged in water-bearing, they sprawled at full length on the steps of the speaker's däis, contentedly munching biscuits.

Canada is *par excellence* the place in which to spend a winter. There are grand clear air, blue sky, and plenty of ice and snow. You do not awake in the morning with the anxious question whether you will that day require a heavy overcoat or an umbrella; the frost is sure and steady, holding from December till the beginning of March,—when the Spring thaw supervenes. In the latter season, Toronto certainly has its drawbacks. As has been the frost, so is the thaw; the melting snow drips in a continuous shower from the house-roofs upon the luckless wayfarer; and the wooden pavements, thoroughly saturated with the wet, steam in the mild air like a universal vapour bath. Wooden pavements, by the way, although poor in appearance, are very pleasant to walk upon, having a spring and elasticity quite wanting in flagstones. They are generally of pine; and the planks being soaked in tar when laid down, last for a number of years. Many of the streets have beds of cedar logs split lengthways and laid across, above which are placed earth and stones to the thickness of a couple of feet. Canada is pre-eminently a "wood" country: stone is scarce and expensive, while wood can be had in any quantity at a low price. Brick is much employed in building, and looks well, as it is much brighter than English brick: but thirty years ago even a brick house was a rarity in Toronto.

The environs of Toronto have a beauty of their own. They are by no means so flat as those of the American cities which we visited; being broken here and there by steep little ravines intersected by brooks, and covered on their sides with large fir trees. Fir woods are widely scattered over the face of the country. Sleighing along a country lane one peaceful evening, we saw one of the most beautiful "bits" we had met with since landing in America. Looking away down the long straight snowy road, fringed with tall pines, we could see the sun setting in the distance, and bathing the end of the vista in a perfect glory of warm mellow light. The surrounding country would not have been unlike "auld Scotland," had it only possessed a background of mountains.

Canada abounds in winter amusements—sleighing, skating, toboggining, snow-shoeing, and many more. The Canadian skating rink is a national institution.

Every town of consequence possesses at least one rink; the finest being capacious brick erections, with glass roofs. The ice being thus covered in is kept free from snow, and the rink is flooded anew every night. In Canada everybody skates well; while in the American cities—notably in Chicago—a really good skater seemed to be the exception. The Yankee rarely snatches time from his business for such recreation; and when he does appear on the ice, he seems quite content if he can only preserve his equilibrium, and proceed straight forwards. But Canadian skating is of the most finished order; the Canadian is a master of his art; advancing, receding, pirouetting, twirling, and threading the most intricate figures with easy grace. He learns to skate almost as soon as he can walk; and accordingly seems in after years to skate as he walks, by intuition. Nor is this proficiency confined to one sex; for Canadian ladies, too, skate with great elegance. We were fortunate enough to see a fancy dress carnival at the Adelaide Street Rink, Toronto, where all sizes and sexes took part. A gallery ran round the upper part of the building, from which spectators looked down upon the lively and changing scene. Every variety of costume, brilliant and sombre, grave and gay, was there; and the spectacle contrasted laughably with a fancy ball, by the frequent mishaps arising from the slippery nature of the floor. An imp in the guise of a Newfoundland dog, hotly pursued by a negro minstrel, would get between the legs of a stately cavalier gliding past with a rosy quakeress, causing his sudden discomfiture and downfall; while a Cistercian monk, coming up from behind with the Queen of Sheba, would come to unutterable grief among the fallen ones, and complete the catastrophe. Curling, too, is a great Canadian pastime; and space is usually set apart on the rink for the devotees of the "roaring game."

Toboggining is not so much pursued in Western Canada as in Montreal. The toboggin is a light sled of very thin wood, made by the Indians, upon which two or more persons sit, and shoot down a snow slope with great velocity. If no track has previously been made down the hill, and the toboggin has thus to rush through soft snow, a blinding cloud is raised, of which the foremost occupant gets the full benefit; so that when the descent is accomplished, his mouth, eyes, ears, and pockets are filled with snow. The man at the rear of the toboggin steers with his foot; and steering requires no small practice, bad management being certain to result in an inglorious "capsize." The chief objection to toboggining is that the toboggin has to be dragged up hill again after each descent.

A very salient point about the Canadian boy is his sled. The visitor will be struck by this—both mentally and on his shins—before being two days resident in Canada. Every youthful Canadian is the possessor of a tiny sled, which he drags after him wherever he goes, and upon which he shoots down every little slope he comes to. He much prefers the public side-walk to an open space of ground, however inviting the latter. When he arrives at the top of a gentle declivity, his mode of procedure is to take a run, pushing his sled before him; then, having attained sufficient impetus, to throw himself on his stomach on the sled and shoot down, generally finishing in the kennel or against a lamp-post. Boys of an enterprising turn frequently impress a retriever or large dog of some kind, and harness it to the sled, upon which they sit in supreme delight, brandishing a whip. We noticed an amusing difference of opinion between one embryo Jehu and his steed, which resulted in the dog bolting off with the sled after a passing horse, leaving his master in a sitting position on a heap of snow by the roadside, bellowing like Lord Ullin at the ferry.

Upon Toronto Bay there are several ice-boats. Opposite the city, about two miles out, lies a long low island, which breaks the force of the wind and waves, so that the large expanse of water inside becomes frozen hard. Hanlan, the redoubted sculler, lives upon the island, and may be seen every day in summer rowing on the bay. The frozen bay offers a fine stretch for the ice-boats, which, from their novelty and speed, cannot fail to attract the stranger. An ice-boat is simply a light wooden framework upon three iron skates or runners, two of those being set forward, and the third at the stern. The last is on a swivel, and being connected with a tiller, acts as the helm. A short mast rises from the stem, on which is hoisted a great lateen sail. During our visit the ice was not in favourable condition, being always covered with broad patches of hard snow; but in spite of this I have seen the ice-boats skimming along in a moderate breeze at twenty miles an hour. Ice-boats can sail wonderfully close to the wind; but their fastest point in a stiff breeze is with the wind fair abeam, when, if the ice be smooth, they sail forty or fifty miles an hour. They do not attain this rate when running before the wind, not being able to go faster than the wind; but with the breeze abeam it is different, and there is then hardly any limit to their speed. But the most noted ice-boats are to be seen at Poughkeepsie, on the Hudson River. The New York Central Railroad runs along the shore of the river, and the boats try daily conclusions with the trains, always passing the latter if there be a proper sailing breeze. The time known to have been made by several of those boats is almost incredible. The "Haze," of Poughkeepsie, has accomplished nine miles in seven minutes. The following are the principal dimensions of the "Icicle," a new craft,—the largest, and supposed to be the fastest ice-boat in the world. Total length, 68 feet. Framework 32 feet in length from mast-step to rudder-post. Width of frame, 6 feet; distance between runners, 26 feet; length of forward runners, 7 feet 6 inches. Length of bowsprit, 25 feet; length of boom, 43 feet; height of mast, 32 feet. Carries 1071 square feet of canvas, No. 7 single duck.

The Toronto people, as befits their hospitable character, are much given to entertaining; and there are several large balls in the course of the winter, with not a few smaller gatherings of a similar nature. But balls and dances sink into obscurity beside a Canadian tea-party, which is a thing by itself. A Canadian tea combines the solid viands of dinner with the more delicate comestibles proper to itself, and is a repast which, if partaken of to its full extent, is likely to provide the consumer with nourishment for a week ensuing. The amusement of the evening is varied; and among other things a usage sometimes obtains which has nearly fallen out of vogue at home—that of recitations. Occasionally these are clever; but there is usually danger of a drawing-room recitation falling rather flat. The number of men who can recite, is considerably more limited than that of those who cannot; and it is always a painful thing to see a man rise with a stolid face, insinuate his left hand beneath his left coat-tail, extend his right heavenwards, and then pointing his right toe and a moral simultaneously, give vent to some awful platitude about the Fall of Man, or the Beneficent Care of Providence over the Tender Hedgehog. The man of philippics is out of place in private life; and Demosthenes, however glorious to the world, cannot have been a comfort to his parents.

In Toronto there is the same cheapness of living which characterises the States. For men engaged in business in the city, whose homes lie at a distance, the boarding-house takes the place of the English lodging. Young men do not engage separate lodgings as in an English town, but club together in numbers of eight or ten to fill up a boarding-house. They take their meals in a common room, but each has a comfortable bed-room, which he can use if he likes as a private sitting-room. For first-class accommodation and food of this kind, the charge is 5 dollars, or £1, per week; and more real comfort is often secured than an English lodging holds out at double the money. By the boarding-house arrangement, too, there is no room for operations on the part of the landlady's cat, which interesting animal may be estimated to cost the British lodger from half-a-crown to five shillings weekly.

We were desirous, while in the west of Canada, of seeing something of life in the backwoods: so it was arranged that Davis and I should make an expedition to the lake and forest country of the northern district, with a young Canadian friend as our guide. We possessed no friend in the backwoods corresponding to our host of Piper City, no acquaintance to whose abode we might direct our steps; so we furnished ourselves with abundance of warm clothing, blankets, and provisions, lest we should be obliged on occasion to make our bed in the woods. Those necessary supplies we lashed upon a large toboggin, purposing to draw the latter after us as we journeyed. And the account of the trip calls for a new chapter.

CHAPTER XIV.

TO THE WOODS.

ON the morning of our start we were astir betimes, got our baggage and toboggin balanced precariously on the top of a cab, and drove to the station of the Northern Railroad of Canada. Our costume was picturesque rather than civilized; we expected a roughish time, and accordingly sacrificed all superfluous vanity. Each man gloried in a well-worn coat, brown canvas trousers or overalls, and a pair of moccasins, the overalls being tucked inside the stockings. Johnson, our Canadian friend, brought with him a Skye terrier, short-haired and short-legged, and known as "Spieach." (The proper way to enunciate this is to emit a hissing sound, and then cough). We deposited our effects in the luggage van, while Johnson, towing the dog by a long string, advanced to purchase a dog ticket.

"What is the name, sir?" asked the ticket official.

"Spieach," replied Johnson gravely.

"Didn't just catch it, sir. What did you say?"

"Spieach," reiterated Johnson, with a bland smile.

"Sp-p-pugh! Remarkable name, sir. Not a Toronto name, I guess?"

"Hardly. It isn't my name—name of the dog. My name is Johnson."

"Ah, I see! Here's the ticket, sir—twenty-five cents."

Our destination was Gravenhurst, a village at the southern extremity of Muskoka lake, a hundred and sixteen miles north of Toronto. As we journeyed on, the country inclined more and more to its native forest; and even in the clearings the tree-stumps had not been uprooted, but appeared black and dismal through the snow. A fellow-traveller in the carriage showed a disposition to become remarkably friendly, pouring forth upon us an irresistible flood of information regarding the district; but as he and his statements laboured under the respective disadvantages of intoxication and inaccuracy, we did not derive signal benefit from his companionship.

At mid-day we reached Gravenhurst, collected our belongings, and packed them forthwith on the toboggin. Then getting the ropes over our shoulders, we dragged away merrily to the lake shore, intending to proceed upon the ice to a shanty some miles up, and there pass our first night. The bank of the lake was high, with a hollow snow-drift piled against it, and it became a question how to get the toboggin safely down to the ice. At last, taking a rope each, Johnson and Davis made a rush. Sinking past the waist in the soft snow, they completely stuck; but the flat-bottomed toboggin, once set in motion down the slope, took the bit in its teeth, and shot cheerily over the wreath on to the lake. The snow on the open ice was only four inches deep, so our labour was not very hard, and we gained the shanty before sundown.

The owner of the mansion was extremely hospitable, and his wife speedily prepared a repast of fried pork, bread, and tea, to which we did ample justice. The shanty was a rude structure of wooden logs, containing two apartments; and though not imposing in point of style, it proved sufficiently warm and comfortable. But in the Canadian bush, the barn altogether takes precedence of the shanty. Capacious in size, being two or three times as large as the dwelling-house, the barn is contemplated by its proprietor with feelings akin to veneration. In it his live stock, consisting probably of a horse, a cow, and a few sheep, are housed for the winter,—the barn likewise representing his granary and hayloft. Both barn and shanty are the work of his own hands; for in the forest the settler does everything for himself. Judging from the singularly unambitious nature of forest architecture, there is here a promising opening for the young architect of refined taste, whose talents may not have met with that appreciation in the city which their excellence merits.

Towards evening, the question arose where we should sleep. Our host and his spouse being blessed with a liberal allowance of olive branches, and the accommodation being none too large, we could not hope for the luxury of beds. Had we been as experienced then as we afterwards became, we would have struck right into the bush, made a fire on the snow, and taken our rest within our blankets; but unhappily we were more ambitious that night. The settler chanced to be erecting close by a new and much more commodious house, so we determined to make this our sleeping quarters. The edifice was of wood, a keen north wind was whistling through the unfinished walls, and there being no stove, we could not light a fire; but, confident in the virtue of sleeping-bags and blankets, we bade defiance to the cold and good night to our entertainer, and composed ourselves to rest. Each one had an eight pound blanket sewn up in the form of a bag, into which to creep for the night; and there being only twenty degrees of frost, we scoffed at the mention of discomfort with such ample provision in the way of clothing. But ere two hours had passed, I was roused from a precarious slumber by sundry discontented ejaculations; and peering through the dim light, I could see a shadowy form, freed from its sleeping-bag, investing itself with every additional article of clothing upon which it could lay its hands. I watched it struggle into a second pair of trousers, with running *sotto voce* complaints as to the difficulty of insertion; next it wrestled with a spare flannel shirt, in the attempt to coax the latter over its already thick habiliments; and lastly assuming a huge comforter and a pair of mittens, it wriggled into its bag again and lay down. Then the consciousness dawned upon myself of an unpleasantly severe sensation—of a cold air that seemed to strike my shoulders and penetrate downwards to my very toes; so, rising from my couch, I followed the spectre's example. But in spite of all the wraps we could put on, we were forced in the morning to confess that our night's rest had not been of the sweetest. No amount of blankets will compensate for the want of a fire. It is better, as we afterwards found, to sleep in the open woods with the temperature much below zero, having a fire at your feet, than to seek repose—even under shelter—without a fire.

A good breakfast next morning set all to rights; and at 8 A.M. we struck out on the ice, with the intention of making our way to Port Carling, a little village at the head of the lake, twenty-two miles off.

The professed object of the whole expedition was to reach a small island on Lake Joseph, some thirty-five miles to the northward, where Johnson was wont to camp out in summer-time. This island boasted a frame house and a hut, both of them deserted in winter; and we proposed taking up our abode in the latter. Our real aim in the trip, however, being only to gain some acquaintance with bush life, we were ready to make any alteration in our plans the better to accomplish this.

Away we started, then, pulling lustily at the toboggin, with the little dog trotting happily in the rear. We had donned our snow-shoes, there being several inches of snow upon the ice,—and Davis and I did not feel quite at home in these appendages at first; but in a very short time we acknowledged their utility. Johnson of course was an adept in their use, pushing along with enormous strides. To a spectator it seems much more difficult to walk in snow-shoes than really is the case. The best way to convince yourself of their benefit is to take them off in deep snow and attempt to progress without them; when the labour will be so increased that you will be glad to resume what you may have deemed encumbrances. In three feet of soft snow a man without snow-shoes will sink to his waist, while with snow-shoes he will not sink more than six inches.

Rounding a point in the lake, we saw our course stretching straight before us for eight miles, at which distance a wooded island rose on the horizon. It was snowing heavily; and the great, white, trackless expanse looked inexpressibly desolate. In the course of the forenoon, however, the weather cleared, and everything quickly became as bright as before it had been dreary; the sun shone out brilliantly,—and so oppressive were its rays, that we threw off our coats and dragged away in our shirt sleeves. Halting for a moment, however, to snatch a rest and have a pull at our pipes, we had speedily to resume the upper garments,—proving that it was only the exertion which induced the heat. The sun cast a strong glare upon the snow, which became very galling to the eyes. (This snow-glare has a strong effect in tanning the complexion.) Reaching the island mentioned, we found it to be only the first of a series, which at this part spread themselves over the lake in an intricate network. This was a very confusing feature; many of the islands were large, and undistinguishable at first from the mainland; while between them opened so many channels, that we had great difficulty in finding our way. Often we advanced through a passage which at first seemed like a narrow bay with apparently no outlet ahead, till on our reaching an unseen corner, the channel would take a sudden bend, and widen out into the lake beyond. Islands grouped in this way are a common feature of the lesser Canadian lakes. But however the islands enhanced the beauty of the scenery, we could not regard them as an unmixed blessing; for the ice in their neighbourhood was so sheltered from the wind, that the snow lay upon it to the depth of a couple of feet. Our snow-shoes kept us well upon the surface; but the heavily laden toboggin sank deeply, and became very hard to draw. At times we came to patches of water ice; the water rising up in our footsteps and in the track of the toboggin. The only plan on arriving at such a place was to "put on steam," and shoot across as quickly as possible. Water ice, or "cat ice" as it is called, is formed by snow falling upon the lake when it first freezes; the snow freezes along with the ice, and produces an imperfect or honeycombed coating. It is not a pleasant thing to find yourself on "cat ice" for the first time, though afterwards you become better accustomed to it. And you come upon it without warning, for the snow covers good and bad ice alike. But it is never safe to cross such ice without snow-shoes, for a man sinking deeply into the slush runs great risk of having his feet frozen afterwards.

When evening fell, we had accomplished only sixteen miles, and were fervently desirous of reaching our journey's end, the heavy load and the deep snow beginning to tell severely. Learning from a settler that there was a shorter path to Port Carling through the woods, we left the lake intending to seek this, and toiled up a steep bank. At the top of the bank stood a shanty; from which, as we were about to pass, there emerged a couple of men, one of whom addressed us—

"You have a stiffish load there, I see. Are you going to Port Carling?"

"That is our intention. Six miles farther, is it not?"

"I should say it was. You had better come in first, and have some tea."

We looked enquiringly at one another. To men in our condition, tea was too good an offer to be refused; and assent seemed written on each face.

"We'll be uncommonly happy, and many thanks to you."

"Leave the load out there, then, and come in."

Following the speaker, we entered the shanty, which consisted of one large room, with some rude furniture and a stove in the centre. Our entertainer, a young man of thirty—and clearly a gentleman, though in the garb of a backwoodsman—busied himself in preparing the meal, while he bade us shake the snow from our garments and make ourselves at home. His companion, a rough looking character, remained a passive (though by no means uninterested) spectator of the culinary preparations. Soon the pork began to crackle in the frying-pan, and the large kettle to sing on the stove, while a grateful aroma of pork and tea diffused itself through the apartment. Half an hour more, and we were seated at the festive board—represented by a deal table; and the clatter of knives and forks upon the tin dishes gave witness that every man was doing his duty. We were too hungry to converse.

"Now," said our host, when at last we desisted, from sheer inability to eat any more,—"light your pipes, and get round the stove. I am going to wash up."

We did so, watching the proprietor of the shanty light the stump of a clay pipe, and proceed to immerse the dishes in a great tin tub of hot water. At length, having finished his task, he seated himself comfortably with his feet on the stove, and proceeded—

"What brings you fellows up to Muskoka at this time of the year? Are you on a hunting trip?"

"We've come up to see the place, and find out how people live in the backwoods."

"Peculiar season to choose for doing it, I must say! Are you from Toronto?"

"I am," replied Johnson; "but the others are Scotchmen — just arrived out. They wanted to try the bush for a bit; so I am taking charge of them."

"Ah, that's the idea, is it? So you have newly come out from the old country?" said our host, looking at Davis.

"Only three months ago."

"It's a pleasant thing to see old country faces up here,—especially in the winter. I am an Englishman myself—good honest Lancashire—as you may find out if you have any knowledge of a Lancashire dialect. If you are Scotch, I hardly suppose you will know anyone in my part of the country?"

"Well," said I, "I know one man there;" naming him. "He married my cousin."

"The dickens he did! Why, I was at school with that very fellow in Preston fifteen years ago. What a rum thing I should have happened to ask you in here to-night!"

"It is very queer, certainly! Well, it only goes to prove that the world is not so very big after all."

"So it does." And he ruminated for a while.

Then addressing his companion—"I say, Zeke, you had better chop some more wood now,—the stove is getting low."

The individual indicated rose in a leisurely manner,

shook himself, and disappeared outside; whence we shortly afterwards heard the strokes of an axe.

"Who is Zeke? Does he live here?"

"Why, he is my man. He chops my wood and draws water."

He doesn't seem to wash the dishes, anyhow!

"Scarcely. You may be jolly sure he won't do anything more than he is obliged to; I have to cook and bake and wash for myself."

"Zeke appears to have no objection to eat, however! Does he always sit with you at table?"

"My good sir, you evidently have not yet succeeded in grasping the idea of bush life. Zeke wouldn't stop with me a day if I refused to let him have his meals with me; all those beggars expect that in the bush. Not that I should particularly object to it, if they were not so abominably lazy otherwise. Zeke never helps me in the house; he knows he is engaged only to chop and carry and do out-door work, and he sticks rigidly to his agreement. But he's not a bad fellow, if you take him the right way."

"Have you been long out here?"

"Seven years now; but I take a run across occasionally to see how things are at home."

"And how do you like the life?"

"I like it very well, and so I just stay on. I used to be in business at home, but this seems to suit me better. It is all a matter of taste, you know,—some men would find it slow; perhaps I may in time, and if I do, I shall go home again. It's a pretty rough thing, as you may see, and there is a trifling lack of variety; but it has its charms. Sometimes I get a little hipped; and then I run down to Toronto or Montreal for a change of scene."

"But you can't have any friends in a place like this? Zeke is all very well as an ornament, but he can't be much in the way of conversation. Don't you feel the want of a few men in your own position badly?"

"I am more fortunate than most in that respect, for there are one or two very good fellows in the neighbourhood. A couple of Liverpool merchants are settled near this, who were unlucky at home; and there are some very decent settlers within range. Why, there are several 'Varsity men in this district."

"You don't say so! All farming, I suppose?"

"Nearly all. I don't do much farming myself, though I have some land: I am more in the lumber trade. I knocked up that little saw-mill you would notice down by the lake, and I keep a gang of men working in the season. They left me only a few days ago."

"Then you are likely to make a better thing of it than if you were simply a farmer?"

"I don't know about that. It is expensive to send my lumber down to market from this out-of-the-way place; and the lumber market is very changeable. A farmer, again, is always pretty sure of a good return from his crops. But the settlers are somewhat lazy; and very few of them do any farming worth speaking of. It doesn't give them much trouble to procure the necessaries of life; and when they have these, they are satisfied."

"People at home suppose that the backwood settler has a very hard time, and that it takes him all he knows to make a living."

"People at home are not infrequently wrong. I will tell you precisely how the thing stands. When an English labourer, we shall say, comes out to an uncleared district, he gets from Government a free grant of a hundred acres, with the reservation that he is to clear twenty acres in five years. At first he has uphill work, and he needs a little capital to start with. He has the expense of building his house and clearing so much land, before his place becomes productive; therefore he needs something to tide him over the first year or so. But once a part of his land is in crops and yielding a return, he has little more trouble, comparatively speaking. Ten pounds will cover his food for a year, and he wants very little for clothes; so when he has cleared his fixed amount he doesn't bother about more, but sits down quietly and takes things easy."

" He might make money, then, if he chose to work."

" So I should say. If he cleared all his grant, he would have a tidy farm; and he might buy as much more uncleared land as he wanted for a dollar an acre."

" Could he not sell his timber too, as he cuts it down?"

" Not very well, unless he made a regular business of it. The time and cost of hauling it down to the lake, and then the transportation to market, would just about wipe off any little profit he might make. The ordinary settler will find it cheaper to burn the timber he can't use."

We sat for some moments in silence, till W——, our entertainer, exclaimed—

" I say, you men had better stay here with me for a day or two. If you would like it, say so; and it will be a mutual benefit. I shall feel quite jolly having you here."

We did not hesitate to close with this hospitable proposal; and we accordingly became the inmates of the shanty for more than a week. During this time, we considerably widened our knowledge of the domestic arts. We learned how to cook and bake,—and also the science of washing dishes; we swept up the floor, and shook down the bunks; and we even attempted tailoring,—at least, if variegating our torn garments with patches from any bit of stuff that came handy, could be said to constitute that art. And we are accordingly disposed to look back on our residence in the shanty with much satisfaction, as a period which enlarged our minds, and taught us practical principles, which, for anything we can tell, may be of great advantage to us in after life!

CHAPTER XV.

THE CANADIAN BUSH.

WE had a very varied experience of life in the bush. After spending some time in W——'s shanty, we extended our trip to its original destination, the island of Yohocucaba on Lake Joseph. To this place W—— and his gifted subordinate Zeke accompanied us, having no special work on hand, and being glad to break the monotony of their daily life. We traversed the icy surface of Lake Rosseau, and then explored Lake Joseph, on which the island was situated. The broad frozen sheet of Lake Joseph looked very waste and dreary, with no sign upon its shores of human habitation, or even of animal life. As we snowshoed over Lake Joseph, Jack confidently advanced the assertion that we had reached the North Pole. Those three lakes, Muskoka, Rosseau, and Joseph, form a continuous chain, being connected with one another by small rivers and artificial openings. One and all bear a considerable resemblance to Loch Lomond, both in their size, and in being thickly studded with wooded islands.

The smaller Canadian lakes abound in charming scenery. The district surrounding is composed of rock and wood, while here and there appear eminences almost deserving the title of hills. But even flat country becomes beautiful if relieved by lake and forest. In the summer and autumn, the Muskoka region is sought by tourists; and parties go up taking tents and all the paraphernalia required for a summer encampment. "Camping out" is a favourite Canadian practice; and the atmosphere being entirely free from humidity, it may be indulged in without dread of rheumatism.

The primeval forest in its winter dress presents an enchanting picture. The tall pines feathered with snow, the deep cloudless blue of the sky, and the almost startling stillness which prevails around, combine to produce an effect on the spectator that can never be forgotten. Comparatively few people are permitted to see Nature in this—one of her sublimest manifestations; and the singular beauty of the Canadian winter woods, as we saw them, will never pass from our recollection.

During our sojourn in the forest, we were the recipients of great hospitality from the settlers. Arriving at a shanty at nightfall, we were warmly pressed to partake of the evening meal, and made welcome to a share of the floor upon which to spread our blankets for the night. We did have some rather peculiar sleeping experiences, certainly. I have formed one of five closely packed on the floor in a ten feet space, I have reposed on an uncertain arrangement of rickety chairs and crazy benches, and I have slept in a shantyman's straw bunk; I have extended my feet beneath the stove, and I have pillowed my head upon a pork ham. But we never underwent such another penance as on that memorable night in the unfinished house!

We found at the outset considerable difficulty in the elaboration of a morning toilet; and were forced in some measure to imitate the example of the bushmen,—who dispense with toilet *in toto*. Lying down to rest at night, we retained our daily clothing, each man merely enwrapping him in a blanket, disposed as an ancient toga. (There is a touching simplicity about bush life.) Our fare was coarse, but always acceptable. Pork and molasses, damper and tea,—tea and damper, pork and molasses; morning, noon, and night, it was ever the same. But with hard strong exercise during the day, we never failed of voracious appetites, attacking the pork and damper as an alderman would abandon himself to turtle and venison.

The toboggin was from first to last an awful incubus. Had the ice been clear, or had there been only a few inches of snow upon it, pulling would have been easy; but from the great depth of snow which covered lake and bush, it was a work of pain and sorrow. Even with the additional help of W—— and Zeke, we often made but tardy progress. Sometimes the toboggin would sink deeply into a drift, when exclamations like the following might be heard ;—

"Yank her along, boys!" from Zeke, in a state of contumely and perspiration.

"Ye—oh—heave—oh!" from Johnson, straining at the rope till his muscles cracked and the veins stood out on his forehead.

"Come up then, will ye!" from Davis, as if addressing an unwilling horse.

"Now then, with a will!" from W——, with a set face that might have done credit to an Olympic wrestler.

Again we would make a portage through the bush, to avoid a patch of open water in a narrow part of the lake. By dint of terrible tugging and shoving, we would get the load to the top of a bank; when, descending the other side, the toboggin would break from control and come to an untimely overturn against a rock or tree, while the goods rolled off in every direction. Procedure in this way was not rapid; so we were fain at length to invoke the aid of a settler with his bullock and sleigh. Transferring the packages from the toboggin to the latter, we advanced on our way with a heartfelt sense of relief. A Canadian bullock is not the least stubborn of animals. Forming its own plan with a praiseworthy conscientiousness, it decides either to remain stationary, or to assume only a retrograde movement; and not until it has been brought to the light of conviction, through the instrumentality of a young sapling, will it join its master in the desired unanimity of purpose. The bullock-sleigh was not an expensive mode of carriage. For twelve shillings its owner conveyed our load a distance of thirty miles; he having of course to retrace the same course with his empty vehicle. A man's wage in the forest is generally reckoned at one dollar fifty cents, or six shillings, per day.

Snowshoeing in the bush is extremely pleasant. At first it is laborious, owing to the nature of the ground; but the novice soon becomes hardened to the exercise. The Canadian forest is like an endless Scotch fir-wood, with a surface broken by scattered rocks and fallen trees; the latter at times piled so closely together as to form a perfect *abattis*. There are constant ups and downs, and steep little banks; and a thick undergrowth thrusts itself unpleasantly upon your notice, by catching the points of your snow-shoes, or whisking off your head-dress and holding it playfully suspended in mid air. If you allow one snow-shoe to tread upon the other, the result is an abrupt stop, and woful downfall. It was pleasing to contemplate Davis after such a catastrophe, fixed in a heavy drift in an inverted position; his most prominent feature to the onlooker being a pair of snow-shoes pointing helplessly heavenward. It is far from easy to regain the perpendicular after a really successful fall in snow-shoes. The man who leads the way has the hardest task, being obliged to make his progress through unbroken snow; while the rest find it comparatively easy to follow in the track which he has beaten down.

Backwoodsmen not infrequently engage in a deer hunt through the bush. Following up the trail of the deer on the snow, they generally succeed in coming up with him in six or seven miles; the deer sinking more deeply than the hunter on snow-shoes, and being therefore unable to run so quickly. This kind of chase is known as "still-hunting."

There is little sport in the Muskoka forest in winter-time beyond still-hunting and rabbit snaring. Muskoka winter rabbits seem just a reproduction of Scotch white hares, but are not found in large numbers. In the summer and fall better sport is to be had; the game which frequent the region at those seasons being chiefly deer, brown bears, partridges, and ducks. Bears are very scarce, and very timid, making off with clumsy haste at the approach of man. The Canadian partridge resembles in size and plumage the grey hen, the mate of the black cock; but unlike the latter it is an exceedingly stupid bird, remaining stationary when discovered, and almost inviting the sportsman's aim. Partridges are found in groups upon the trees, and slaughtered in that position;—but some excuse is found for this unsportsmanlike proceeding in the closeness of the foliage, which would render flying shots extremely difficult. Besides the game mentioned, foxes, skunks, squirrels, and the like abound; a few of those being valuable to the trapper on account of their skins. The lakes teem with fish; the best kind being bass, which bite readily, and are not hard to capture. In addition to those larger expanses whose frozen surfaces we traversed, the bush is continually interspersed with smaller lakes or ponds, each with its little outlet or creek.

Moccassins are indispensable for winter work in the forest. They are the only coverings which really serve to keep the feet warm, and the only articles suitable for snow-shoes. The moccassin is an Indian device, made of soft untanned leather, and rising round the ankle in broad flaps secured by thongs.

It has no heel. Acting solely as a protection, it does not embarrass the foot, but stretches itself exactly to the shape of the latter, so that the foot is to all intents as free and unconfined as if it were bare. The moccassin is the most perfect appliance known, being more easy and natural, if less elegant, than the orthodox boot. Two or three pairs of socks are worn; and backwoodsmen occasionally insert a layer of brown paper into the moccassin, the paper being peculiarly impervious to cold. In slush or wet snow, moccassins would quickly become soaked; but in the long Canadian winter slush is unknown, never appearing until spring. Why the prairie settlers of the Western States have not adopted moccassins, is an unanswered question; for the moccassin is beyond comparison more serviceable in snow than the high leather boot.

The cold in the bush is demonstrated by the thermometer to be intense; but it seldom feels severe, owing to the absence of wind. I have been upon the lake in a blustering, piercing north-easter that seemed to freeze the very marrow; and then, striking a hundred yards into the forest, I have found everything calm and still, without the sensation of a breeze. The woods afford a most perfect shelter; and by lighting a fire and rolling yourself in blankets, you may sleep as soundly on the snow as upon a feather bed. We passed a night in the woods when the thermometer indicated twenty-four below zero, and found it hard to believe that the temperature was in fact so low. And I have seen Zeke, that redoubted servitor, seated by the camp fire at night with no clothing save his trousers and a woollen undershirt,—the latter widely open at the neck.

The plan of action in camping out is to select a spot at the foot of a bank, and cut down a small tree. An axe is an indispensable companion in the forest. Splitting the tree into four feet lengths, you place those upon the snow as the basis of a fire; and then collecting a quantity of small dry branches, you lay them on the top and initiate a blaze. The fire is fed with great logs which you hew from the fallen tree and pile on as required. You break off a number of green pine boughs, and freeing them from their load of snow, dispose them as your couch; when they are found to possess a grateful elasticity comparable only with a spring mattress. Then the tea is boiled in the camp kettle, while each expectant consumer impales his junk of pork upon a stick, and fries it to suit his special liking. After the meal follow pipes, songs, and stories; and at an early hour the party creep into their blankets, and seek repose. On awaking in the morning, the fire is found to have sunk down two or three feet below the surface of the gradually melted snow.

In our rambles through the bush, Zeke was a mirth-provoking spectacle. Sometimes as I gazed on him stalking on in front, I was so overcome with laughter as to be forced to pause till I regained my gravity and my breath. He was conspicuous by an ancient Jim Crow hat, with the band worn to a fringe, a ragged tail coat, many sizes too small and short for his strapping frame, and a pair of inexpressibles—which literally bore out the title. In his tail was stuck a tomahawk, and upon his shoulder he proudly carried a rifle;—though he seldom found anything to shoot. And with a naturally shambling gait (not improved by the snow-shoes), he presented a *tout ensemble* far beyond the power of pen to depict. His character was no less original than his appearance; and I was more than once privileged to engage him in conversation.

"Zeke," I said to him one evening, as he sat beside the stove mending his moccasin,—"have you always lived up here in Muskoka?"

"Skurcely," replied that hero. "I'se been a heap o' things afore I come here. I'se been trapper, an' river-driver, an' paddler, an' a sight o' things beside. Trappin's my reg'lar business; I allus goes out in the fall. I'se goin' to lie out on Moon River next fall for mink and foxes."

"Can you make much money by trapping?"

"That's all as regards the luck I'se get. Ef I kin strike a good saison and plenty o' skins, I'se come out with two or three hunderd dollars. But trappin's a mighty chancy trade. Ef trappin's bad, I go river-drivin'."

"What is that?"

"Raftin', for sure. Takin' the logs down the big rivers in the rafts."

"Ah, I see. That ought to be a more certain business than trapping."

"Wall, I'se allus sure o' my wage; but it's kinder rough work too. Thar's too many o' them ornery Frenchmen at it. Them French Canadians is a blamed mean lot; they'se tarr'ble jealous o' the English."

"What makes them jealous?"

"They'se poor workers alongside o' the English, an' the English has a bigger wage. Then thar's rows an' fights continual."

"I should think you could settle the Frenchmen pretty well, if it came to fighting."

"O' coorse we can, an' so we do; an' that makes it main nasty workin' wi' them. The French boys never start to fightin' onless they'se two or three to wan agin us; an' they try all kind o' mean tricks. It's wrastlin', an' kickin', an' bitin', an' scratchin'—jest what we call a reg'lar rough an' tumble fight. I mind fixin' two big French lads down on the Ottawa river. They'se set on to me wan night in a lonesome place;—wall, I ketched one boy a blow on the side o' the head as felled him in his tracks, so the other was for movin' off; but I stood to him, so he was boun' to fight. Wall, we played away kinder for a spell, till he made a dab at my eye wi' his finger for to gouge it out; so I jest opened my mouth an' ketched his finger an' bit on to it, an' kicked him in the stummick. I tell ye I'se fixed that French lad proper!"

"A singularly refined style of fighting, I must say!"

"It's jest the reg'lar Canadian style—none o' yer fists on the river, but a rale rough an' tumble fight—take a man as ye'se can git him—that's the sort. But a bar-room fight's the kind o' sport the Frenchmen likes; they'se ketch wan o' us—or maybe two—in a saloon, an' make a rush. Now I'se tell ye the thing for to do is jest to grip as many chairs as ye'se can, an' git behind them in a corner;—then ye'se swing wan around an' smash the other lads on the head. Thar's nary a French boy can say he's bettered me yet."

Zeke was rather given to boasting, and his statements had to be taken with some reservation; but we derived a great deal of amusement from listening to his yarns. He developed a strong individuality in all his proceedings; I recollect his wakening Johnson from slumber one morning by sending a revolver bullet through the wall of the shanty, within eighteen inches of the sleeper's head!

The appearance of a small backwoods village in the depth of winter is not inviting. Emerging one day from the forest in the neighbourhood of Port Carling, and descrying the little hamlet through a veil of thickly falling snow, we were struck by its bleak and dreary look. The rude frame houses stood detached from one another at irregular intervals, each in bare cold relief against the snow. They were small, low, and destitute alike of symmetry and paint. (It is wonderful how greatly a coat of white paint assists the idea of civilization.) Gazing on such a settlement, the spectator at first finds it difficult to associate any thought of comfort with the apparent desolation; still, on entering the shanties, he will find them to possess the material elements of comfort, viz., fire, food, and shelter. Nor does the settler ask more; he is not given to consult appearances; resting content with those common necessaries which can be obtained with the smallest trouble. In this little hamlet, however, we were impressed by the prevalence of churches. No less than four did it contain, although there might not have been more than forty houses in its whole extent. The churches were queer little buildings, distinguishable from the surrounding dwellings only by a more limited size, and a greater appearance of poverty. The settler is denominational rather than devout. He will not unite with his neighbours in a common brotherhood, to secure for his village one resident clergyman; but prefers to erect a preaching-box—the Port Carling churches were nothing more—for his own special form of worship, and rest dependent on the chance visitations of passing pastors.

But Port Carling is a specimen of the smaller backwoods settlements only. On our homeward route we passed through Bracebridge, a place of considerably more importance, and bearing in the character of its trade and in its business activity a close resemblance to Piper City. It possessed several streets of commodious stores; all apparently of wood, excepting a solitary brick establishment. In Bracebridge we soon discerned that we were in a commercial atmosphere—meeting with travellers who had penetrated upwards from the warehouses of the large cities; and so keen did business competition appear, that men from Montreal, four hundred miles distant, vied with the Toronto representatives in pushing their goods.

But Bracebridge differed materially from Piper City, in respect of its possessing an aristocracy. It boasted an Upper Ten—or, to speak more correctly, an Upper Seven; (for we learned that out of its fourteen hundred inhabitants, seven only had attained to this coveted eminence). Those immortal Seven, consisting probably of the largest publicans and storekeepers, were said to look down with ineffable disdain on their humbler neighbours,—and especially on the surrounding settlers, or " bush-whackers."

Bracebridge will ever retain its place in our memories by reason of its " North American Hotel." At this hostelry we were boarded and lodged for the inconceivable sum of one dollar or four shillings per day, receiving food and accommodation as excellent, if not as elaborate, as in a first-class city establishment. The necessaries of life are indeed cheap in Canada ; a fact which should appeal suggestively to our own poorer classes at home. At Gravenhurst hotel, again, we got for one shilling each a dinner of three courses, a glass of beer, and a drive to the railway station in the hotel conveyance,—Johnson, in fact, having a cigar thrown in ; (but this we attributed to his more than commonly pleasing appearance and winning manner).

At length, after many ramblings over wood and lake, we bade a regretful adieu to this rude but strangely attractive life, and retraced our way to Toronto, pondering over what we had seen. And a short space devoted to moralising may not be out of place.

The backwoodsman's is a grand free life, possessing peculiar charms for those who pursue it. External Nature, which has often so great, though possibly unconscious, a power over the mind for happiness or depression, presents itself in the forest in a specially happy phase; the alternation of rock, tree, and water being as far removed from the changeless monotony of the Western prairie, as the hurrying river from the stagnant pond. The rough settler might not admit to himself so delicate a companionship with Nature; but transplant him to a busy city, there to pass the remainder of his days,— and he will speedily pine for the familiar rustle of his forest boughs, and the laughing ripple of his lake. But if the life as it now stands be inviting, it might become doubly so. The backwoodsman, unlike the denizen of the prairie, shews a considerable disposition to laziness. Content, as our friend W—— affirmed, if he can secure the bare necessaries of life— and finding those after the outset attainable without extraordinary exertion, he is disposed to stop short, and seek no more. Satisfied with mere existence, he does not follow after prosperity. The greater part of his allotment remains uncleared, and his frame hut is improved by few of those amenities which might so easily be procured.

I am led to this view, by having witnessed in the bush examples of a precisely opposite state of things. Entering a pretty two-storeyed frame house, I have been ushered into a pleasant parlour, with a piano, neat furniture, and tasteful engravings and water-colour drawings. The owners of this place were certainly not ordinary settlers—being English people of good position, whom limited means had induced to seek a home in the forest; still, what they had achieved with such gratifying success, the backwoodsman might accomplish in his own degree; and might, by a fuller use of his advantages, materially better his circumstances.

The bush, however, is not so well suited to the poorer emigrant as the province of Manitoba. Time forbade our visiting the regions of the Far North-West; but we were enabled to learn something of their character. The land in Manitoba being free from wood, the settler is there able to enter upon agriculture without being obliged to face the preliminary obstacle of clearing. The soil of that province is rich, and its fertility practically unbounded. Emigrants from all parts of Canada itself are daily tending to Manitoba; scarcely a week, indeed, elapsed, without our observing in the newspaper the departure of an emigrant train from one or other of the older Canadian towns. Canada offers a vast field for emigration. Those who seek it, must, however, bear clearly in mind that their industry will be directed to the tillage of the soil. Poverty-stricken tradesmen need not enter Canada in the hope of finding employment there in their accustomed trades. The country is at present encumbered with tradesmen. Before more artisans can be required, a much increased population is necessary; accordingly, the greater the number of emigrants who go out directly to the soil, the speedier and wider will be the future opening for mechanics.

The poorer classes in Britain need not plead inexperience in agriculture as a bar to emigration; Manitoban farming is of that rough-and-ready description which may be mastered in a season. Elaborate tillage is uncalled for; the singular fertility of the soil ensures that the rudest of ploughing and seeding will be followed by plentiful reaping.

While not affirming over-population to be the sole cause of the present distress in Britain—deeming the latter, in fact, to result largely from the stubborn folly of the working-classes,—I am yet of opinion that emigration stands out as the most practicable solution of our difficulty; and the more quickly Government recognises this, by providing our unemployed population with greater facilities in the shape of free passages and pecuniary assistance at the commencement, the better. Though a large sum may be thus expended in promoting emigration, it will cancel itself by the corresponding diminution of poor-rates and relief funds. English workpeople are naturally reluctant to leave their native land; but did they know the comfort of livelihood in Canada, they would not so long hesitate. But the intending emigrant must remember that the soil, and not the city, will be his field of labour.

And not to the lower British orders only do these remarks apply. Persons of better position, who are daily proving at home the increasing difficulty of the problem how to make the ends meet, will find emigration no less, but rather more, to their advantage. Bringing with them to the new country a small capital, they will find their money more productive when laid out in the purchase and tillage of land, than in a precarious commercial venture at home. To the arable or stock farmer, possessed of a little means, the cleared lands of Canada present signal advantages. Emigration from the old country must come with time; the earlier it is adopted, the better will it be both for those who go, and those who remain.

CHAPTER XVI.

THE BAY OF QUINTE, AND THE STONE CITY.

ON the Grand Trunk Railway ;—and this time speeding eastwards—bound to the residence of a friend upon the Bay of Quinte, a large inlet of Lake Ontario, between Belleville and Kingston.

Sleighing up from the railway station, we alighted before a large rambling building, which, from the material of its construction, brought before our minds a flitting recollection of our Muskoka pilgrimage: but any such idea was dispelled on our passing the entrance, for our friend's house, albeit of wood, was conspicuous within by that tasteful finish which marks an American interior. American furniture is light and pretty, the numerous kinds of wood indigenous to the country affording a wide variety for selection. The American lady likes pleasant and tasteful surroundings; and seems (if I may be permitted to remark it) comparatively free from the painful solicitude of her British sister lest articles should be spoiled.

During a month's residence with our friend, we had every opportunity of becoming acquainted with the most pleasant side of Canadian country-house life. While the frost lasted, the sleigh was in daily requisition, the frozen bay holding out great inducements to this pastime; and we were privileged also to taste the delights of a "straw-ride." The latter, being unfamiliar to the less favoured Briton, demands an explanation. On a clear starry night, ten or twelve fun-loving spirits of both sexes embark on a lumber sleigh, and drive away under the broad Canadian moon. Each one seeks at an unguarded moment to precipitate his or her neighbour off the sleigh into the snow, while every fresh *contretemps* is hailed with peals of merry laughter. The horses proceed at an unvarying jog-trot, so that the fallen ones have to gather up themselves and their wits with all due speed and hurry after the sleigh,—reinstated on which, they are either unceremoniously overthrown again, or prevail in turn to eject their persecutors. (Can it be that from thus elbowing a comrade into the snow may have arisen the expression "to give one the cold shoulder?")

Towards the middle of March the frost gave way, the sun's rays beat down with excessive power, and we began to understand the full meaning of the term "slush." Then came showers of Spring rain, calling up to our minds endearing thoughts of our native land; while the pleasure of sallying out once more beneath a humid sky, and being thoroughly drenched, seemed almost too acute for expression. Closely succeeding upon this phenomenal change advanced a reign of mud. Everything became mud—and mud of the most realistic description; the fields were mud, and the roads were mud; while the pedestrian, after a two mile walk, presented all the characteristics of a mud image.

The sleigh being now discarded and relegated to its summer quarters, the buggy is led forth in its place. The buggy is a vehicle of aërial construction, very suggestive of an elongated tea-tray set upon high, light wheels; while in wet or sunny weather a tall leather awning rises up from behind, like the cover of a child's perambulator. But the buggy, from its superior lightness and the strength of its springs, is admirably suited to the nature of its work. Canadian country roads would be perfect but for two features—a prevailing inequality of surface, and a total innocence of Macadam. Those drawbacks have the effect of making the roads mud-beds in spring, and dry water-courses in summer. In winter the highways appear at their best, their management being then taken out of the hands of the trustees by circumstances of an elemental nature. Heavy falls of snow provide a level surface, and sleighing is both easy and pleasant. But in spring and summer a heavy English dog-cart would become helplessly imbedded in the mud, or be shaken to pieces by the ruts from its tight and unyielding construction.

There is an American custom in driving, which is apt to give the Englishman a little trouble before he becomes used to it. On meeting another horse or vehicle, the Yankee keeps to the right hand instead of the left; a practice which seems scarcely so good as our own, since, by our plan, the drivers of the two carriages, being each seated on the right-hand side of their boxes, are brought immediately together in the act of passing, and have thus a better opportunity of judging the nicest space they can allow, in the event of a "close shave" being necessary. Transatlantic riding-horses are trained to canter; and it is difficult when on horseback to modulate the pace to a trot. The persuasive vocabulary employed for their instigation consists of the two ejaculations, " Git ehoop!" and " G'lang ; " the first being the plebeian mode of encouragement, while the second is in every-day use amongst the highest circles.

There are a number of Indians round the Bay of Quinte; but not until their nationality was specially indicated, did we recognise them as differing greatly in appearance from the settlers. The latter are bronzed and tanned to the colour of leather; while the Indians, having intermarried for a number of years past with the whites, have lost much of their original copper hue. The veritable red-skin is now to be found only on the Western frontier. The half-breeds—for such they are—who dwell upon the shores of the Bay of Quinte, dress in the same way as the white men; though a squaw may often be distinguished by some flaring piece of colour in her attire. The Indians receive an annuity from Government, doing only so much additional work as may enable them to eke out a scanty means of subsistence. Government, when buying up the land from their forefathers, did not pay over the purchase money, but placed it at interest; doling out to the Indians their allowance in monthly instalments, to be continued to their descendants in perpetuity. In the event of an Indian marrying and having a family, his annuity is subdivided, every member of the household receiving a fixed share. Suggesting to my informant that some difficulty might attend this plan as time rolled on and the people multiplied, I was reminded that the Indians do not multiply, but appear rather to be dying out. The red man will before many years be a memory of the past, like the mastodon and the ichthyosaurus. Nor does this prospect seem to exercise a very saddening influence upon society; for the Indians are incurably lazy, of dirty habits, and little to be depended upon. " Treacherous" is the term everywhere applied to them.

A soft-hearted philanthropist, in an outburst of generous feeling, once exclaimed to a shrewd Western American—

" Is it not, my dear sir, a painful thought that year by year the poor red man is being driven nearer and nearer towards the setting sun?"

"Wall," replied the American reflectively, " I calc'late it *is* rayther rough on the settin' sun!"

No one entertains any hope of ultimately raising the Indians, socially or intellectually; everybody, on the contrary, judging it to be the best thing that they should gradually fade out, as they appear to be doing. It is a much more hopeful task to elevate the negro than the Indian. The negro, though in natural capacity much inferior to the Indian, is teachable—even desirous to learn; while the Indian is totally apathetic, showing no desire whatever for improvement. The reason probably is, that the Indians are, heart and soul, nomads, as were their fathers before them; and no thoroughly nomadic race has ever risen to a prominent position on the page of history. The Arabs possess much natural nobility of character, with keen and ready minds; yet they have never advanced. Any life other than a roving one appears slowly to kill off both Arab and Indian;

whereas the negro exults in the dignity of being "a man and a brudder," and attains his highest happiness when invested with the lofty silk hat and green neckcloth (with a brass breast-pin) of civilization.

The Indians are regarded by Government in the light of children; they are protected by law, and receive their annuities; but they neither have—nor seem to wish for—any voice in the affairs of the country, being content to live and die as they are. If an Indian were transferred to the city, and there placed in a position of trust and importance, he would either take to whisky and die miserably; or else be descried in the grey light of some fine morning stealing away in a "bee line" for the woods, with no *impedimenta* save his tomahawk and tobacco-pouch.

At last, having exhausted our limit of time (although not the hospitality of our entertainers), we left the Bay of Quinte; Davis turning his face towards Scotland, and I proceeding in single blessedness to Kingston. " Remote, unfriended, melancholy, slow," seemed a description not unsuited to my sense of bereavement — and the progress of the Grand Trunk Railway. Late in the evening the train stopped in an Egyptian darkness and a pool of water; and I was told that we had reached Kingston. Delivering my portmanteau to an expectant cabman, I followed him through a waste place suggestive of

Bunyan's Slough of Despond, till we arrived at his conveyance,—which was a genuine old country "fever-box," albeit dignified and drawn by two horses. After depositing me inside, Jehu rushed off into the night in the hope of securing another fare, (a Kingston station cabman will take as many persons as his cab will hold) ; and I heard him away in the distance shouting for custom, and proclaiming loudly as an inducement, that he had a gentleman already, who would be lonesome without company! Kingston possesses an excellent railway station ; but for some unexplained cause we were brought in as described.

Kingston is not a lively place. It is frequently known as the "Stone City," the houses being for the most part of a bluish-grey stone, which is quarried in the vicinity ; and it rejoices in the usual number of public buildings,—none of which, however, were sufficient to inspire me with rapture. It has two important educational establishments—a University and a Penitentiary; and it boasts besides a military college, conducted on the same principles as Woolwich and Sandhurst. Many young Canadians pass a couple of years in this institution, even though not meaning to follow out a military career ; and appear to derive both benefit and enjoyment from the course. Strong fortifications, in the shape of earth-works and thick martello-towers, mark Kingston as one of the principal military points upon the frontier line dividing the States and Canada. A British garrison was until lately quartered in the city; but since the British troops have been withdrawn from the Dominion, Canada reposes for her protection on the valour of her militia. A large detachment of the latter are stationed in Kingston; and the vision of red-coats sprinkling the city streets seemed familiar and home-like.

During the American war of 1812, Kingston was an important naval depôt, and the scene of an amusing—though expensive—Admiralty fiasco. A United States flotilla, composed of small vessels suited to the character of the waters, had become very offensive by repeated raids on British shipping and British interests, till it was deemed necessary to take some decisive measures for its destruction. Then John Bull, with that eminent sagacity which even yet characterises his conduct of naval affairs, set about building in Kingston a hundred-and-twenty gun ship. When completed, she was probably the most costly vessel at that time in the British navy; for, though her material was easily procured from the adjacent forests, her guns and stores had all to be brought from England, and dragged laboriously up country from Montreal by means of bullocks. Her construction was naturally a lengthy process; while all the time the Americans were continuing to harass our shipping, and, with more practical sense, were turning out from their yard at Sacket's Harbour additional small craft. Some of the latter were known to be begun and finished in the incredible space of six weeks! By the time the "St Lawrence"—for such was the name of the great ship—was launched, the short war was virtually at an end; and the Admiralty found that instead of a mighty engine of devastation, they had become possessed of a white elephant. The unwieldy "St Lawrence" proved of no use on the confined lake; and the question came simply to be, how best to get rid of her. For many years she lay submerged at the entrance to Kingston harbour; till at last her hull was sold to a brewer for £25, on condition that he should raise and remove it. This he succeeded in doing, towing the hulk across the bay to his own place, where the mighty "St Lawrence" was converted into a brewer's wharf. *Sic transeunt gloria mundi*—and the money of the British tax-payer.

Kingston is the head-quarters of Lake Ontario yachting. Canadian yachts, like the larger sailing vessels employed in the inland marine carrying trade, are built on the centre-board principle. Strolling into a builder's yard, I saw a number of those yachts about to be launched for the summer campaign, and had some conversation with the builder.

"What are the special advantages," I asked, "which induce you to adopt the centre-board principle so largely on this side of the Atlantic?"

"Why, centre-board boats are much more suited to our waters than standing keels. The winds here are usually light, and the waters smooth; and a centre-board will run clean away from a standing keel in these circumstances. You see a centre-board is very broad, so she don't sink into the water like an English boat, but sits on the surface like a duck. We call these broad, light-draught yachts 'skimming-dishes.'"

"I wonder how our boats would succeed on the American lakes?"

"They wouldn't do at all, sir,—especially for racing; they would never sail beside a 'skimming-dish' in a light wind; and they would be often running aground in the shallow parts of the lake."

"You ought to see the English boats before judging so decidedly against them."

"I have only come back from the old country quite lately, and I was looking at them carefully when I was there. They are lovely craft, sir, and just suited to your shores, with splendid power in heavy weather and chopping tideways; but they would do no good against our yachts in smooth water and moderate breezes. Look at this ten-tonner now; she is a prize boat, and a perfect model for light weather."

"Is that a ten-tonner? Why, she is no longer than an English five!"

"Twenty-eight feet measurement, sir, from stem-post to stern—that's her length: but look at her beam —eleven feet. You observe she is fine forward, carrying the breadth well aft. That yacht will draw under two feet of water with her centre-board hauled up."

"I suppose her best point is when running down the wind?"

"No; our boats are best close-hauled. We drop the centre-board going to windward, and the ship is so beamy that she don't heel over much, but stands right up to it, and holds every breath she gets."

"I fancy you don't carry much ballast on board?"

"Two tons, sir, iron and sand; and a pile of sand-bags on the weather side of the deck. We are allowed to shift ballast in Kingston,—though it's certainly a wrong principle."

"The absence of lead ought to cheapen the price of the boat very materially?"

"A racing ten-tonner costs about six hundred dollars; and a five, two hundred and fifty."

"That is a very great difference from prices at home."

"Well, the wood is cheap here; and the finish of our yachts is not up to the English. American pine, too, is very light, which just suits the requirement for buoyancy. But some of the Yankee yachts are lighter still; they want them as light as possible for racing, and often build them of hemlock wood; but then they don't last long."

"I suppose you carry a big press of sail?"

"Very fair, sir,—mainsail, topsail, and a large jib, reaching to the head of the mast, which we haul in from the bowsprit end when running, and spread on a spinnaker boom. We don't use a foresail, but only the one large jib."

"It must be a thundering jib!"

"That ten-tonner's jib will measure twenty-one feet along the foot; and her mainsail is twenty-eight feet hoist, with a thirty-four feet boom. It's quite a handsome spread of sail. I wish you could see one of our yachts on the water, sir; you would say she was really a pretty sight."

A short stay sufficed for Kingston: and Ottawa, the seat of the Dominion Legislature, became the next point of attraction.

CHAPTER XVII.

OTTAWA.

"What do they think of us in Britain?"

My questioner was a Canadian about thirty, seated along with myself in the reading-room of the Russell House, Ottawa.

"Why, really, I never thought of asking at home; I came out to see for myself."

"Exactly," said he, with some bitterness;—"people in Britain either take no concern about us at all, or else set us down right away as barbarians."

"My dear sir," I replied, "surely you are labouring under some misconception. In fact, I don't quite understand what you mean."

"I mean to say that you take no interest in us as a people; and you imagine that we are rude and only half civilized. Now, we have in Canada as good a style of living"—

"Unquestionably"—

"And as able public men"—

"I don't doubt it. Where can you have picked up such extraordinary ideas of the English people? Have you ever been in England?"

"Never."

"I fancied so. Then your best plan will be to go across, and form your opinion afterwards. As far as I can judge, people at home regard you with all proper respect; and your feeling of wounded pride is quite uncalled for."

"No, sir; it won't do. You, perhaps, may have the sense to see us in our true light; but your regular Englishman does not. I've met plenty of them travelling here; and they go around with a patronising air, finding fault with everything."

"Ah, yes; the British snob. Unfortunately not an uncommon species; but we don't count him as a responsible being."

"That may be,—still you must allow that in the old country your men are haughty and reserved, and your women stiff and cold as ice."

"My dear sir, I can't allow anything of the sort. You must have been poisoning your mind with some of those Western American newspapers: I know the style of article; it's written chiefly in capital letters, and reads like this:—

"'The English Man is the Unnatural Offspring of a Diseased Social State, elevated upon the Pedestal of his own Blind Self-sufficiency, from which in his Loathsome Pride he surveys Creation through an Eye-glass, with an air of Monarchical Conceit and

Pampered Superiority, considering himself in his Insulated Ignorance to be the Hub of the 'Tarnal Universe. The English Woman—'"

" There, that's quite enough ;—I'm not so bad as that. What I mean to say is, that the British people think we live quite in a different way from them; and don't know much of the comforts and refinements of life."

" Then you are wrong again; for we don't think anything of the kind. But if you will permit me, I'll make a remark. Both you and the Americans talk of being careless of opinion, and of 'doing as you guess please'; still I have noticed both Canadian and Yankee uncommonly anxious to know what English people think of them. Now, would this not indicate that you yourselves have more real pride than the Englishman; for people at home don't much care what other nations think,—though they are not loud in proclaiming their indifference?"

" I guess, sir, we are becoming too philosophical; so we'll quit the subject. Have a cigar?"

Ottawa stands upon a gentle eminence between two rivers, the Ottawa and the Rideau. The city occupies a pleasant position in the centre of an undulating country; the surrounding slopes being covered with stretching belts of forest. At the time of my visit, the heat was very great. A good deal of ice still remained on the Ottawa river—so much so, indeed, that navigation had not opened for the season; still, to judge from the temperature, we seemed to have leaped right into the middle of summer. I touched upon the subject of the heat to a resident in the place; when he quickly said,—

"Heat, sir! This isn't heat. If you stop in Ottawa another month, you will feel heat!"

I shuddered; and said I would take an early opportunity of leaving.

Ottawa owes its fame to the Parliament Houses. These are vast grey stone buildings, of a highly ornate type, and very handsome, both as regards exterior and interior. The Dominion Parliament, like the United States Congress, consists of two Houses, the Legislative Council and the Representatives. Attending the daily deliberations of these bodies, I had ample opportunity of listening to Canadian oratory, and invariably left the Chambers much stifled and edified; the warmth both in the Houses and in the debates being of no common order.

The new protective tariff had for some time been engaging political attention; and statesmen were busied in wrangling out its smaller items, determining the precise amount of duty to be imposed upon each article of import. This augmented tariff (which can be but ephemeral), has sprung from a variety of causes. The finances of the Dominion being scarcely in a flourishing condition, and the Conservative party desirous of office, protection was advanced by the latter as a stalking-horse, under cover of which they succeeded in gaining a majority. Their arguments were in the stereotyped fashion: Canadian farmers were assured of unbounded prosperity, were the market closed to American supplies; moribund manufacturers were promised a new lease of life, by the exclusion of foreign piece goods; and to the country generally was held out a larger revenue, without increased taxation. The much vexed question of reciprocally lowered duties with the United States was dragged forward. Brother Jonathan was struggling to reduce his own abnormal imposts; he ought to be encouraged in his laudable endeavours, and spurred to faster progress by the elevation of the Dominion tariff. The Canadian people—while possibly not accepting these pledges in the same spirit of unbounded confidence in which they were uttered—reasoned thus: "The country is in a bad state; it can scarcely be made worse: let us have this new tariff,—and if it does no good, it will not at least do any harm." So Sir John Macdonald and his party were returned, rather surprised, it is said, at the readiness with which their *ruse* had succeeded;

while the inhabitants of the Dominion are now fully occupied in finding out their mistake.

Sir John Macdonald, the Conservative Premier, bears in personal appearance an extraordinary resemblance to Lord Beaconsfield; though he does not possess a like mastery of eloquence—and the dictionary. His forte lies less in oratory than in the leadership of a party. Mr Alexander Mackenzie, Sir John's great Liberal opponent, is one of the most sterling politicians of the Dominion, eminent for practical sense, great memory, and a wonderful command of details; the assertion having indeed been ventured, that no one has yet successfully combatted Mackenzie on a matter of fact. As a speaker he is hardly brilliant, delivering his opinions in a pronounced Doric monotone.

A large proportion of the Canadian assemblies are Frenchmen from the eastern provinces,—who usually employ their native tongue in parliamentary debate; and the knowledge of French not being adjudged a necessary qualification for candidature, many members are thus unable to understand their brethren's remarks. To have two totally different languages in the same legislative assembly is, to say the least of it, rather undesirable.

The Ottawa Parliament Library is exceedingly handsome, though less extensive than the Washington collection. On the way to this apartment I passed the smoking-room, through the open door of which was visible a full complement of law-givers. My attendant, noting the direction of my glance, smiled broadly, and pointing towards the apartment with his thumb, remarked confidentially, " There's always a quorum in there!"

The Russell House was filled to overflowing with members, so that its entrance-hall became at certain seasons of the day a thorough Parliamentary lobby; while the hotel bar derived a particularly brisk custom from convivial legislators.

A short distance outside of the city is situated Rideau House, the residence of the Governor-General of the Dominion. As is the case with the President of the United States, it is customary to call upon His Excellency: but the mode of procedure in Ottawa is somewhat more befitting. Rideau House, though not a palatial structure, lies in pleasant grounds of park and wood, and is approached by a long avenue. On entering, the visitor is confronted by an orderly with a pen ("the pen is mightier than the sword"), and duly requested to inscribe his name in the visitor's book; after which the ceremony is complete, and the caller retires, impressed by a subdued sense of awful—because unseen—grandeur.

While fully recognising the worth of her present Viceroy, as well as that of his predecessors, Canada frequently recalls the memory of Lord Dufferin, whom she appears almost to have idolised. Able in politics, genial in society, and hospitable to a degree, Lord Dufferin won golden opinions from all; spending his money when in office like a genuine Irishman, and bidding farewell to the Dominion with a light purse and a full heart. A " mark of respect and esteem," (to use the copybook phraseology of civic appreciation), has been raised to his honour in a fine life-size painting hung in the great corridor of the Parliament House.

Apart from politics, the chief industry of Ottawa is lumber, the city being the principal centre of the lumber trade of Ontario. The town of Hull, which is virtually a part of Ottawa—being separated from the latter only by the river, is infamous for the manufacture of matches. The term is used advisedly, for neither Canadians nor Americans have as yet succeeded in turning out a respectable match; confining their efforts to the production of the old-fashioned sulphur lucifer. Many of these matches will scarcely strike fire except upon the trousers (which, however, is the approved transatlantic plan of ignition); while, after obtaining a light, one is compelled to suspend his breath and shut his eyes until the brimstone has burned out. Then, just as he proceeds to use the remains of the match, it becomes extinct. In all of which there appears room for improvement.

Ottawa is also distinguished as being the northern termination of the Rideau Canal. This canal was constructed fifty years ago, for strategic rather than commercial purposes, to facilitate the transportation of military stores from the sea-board to the stations on Lake Ontario. The shortest route from Montreal to Kingston is of course by the river St Lawrence; but as this stream forms the frontier line between Canada and the States, material in process of transit by its channel would have been eminently liable to molestation by the enemy. Desirous, therefore, of possessing for their stores a water-way wholly through Canadian territory, the military authorities planned the Rideau Canal; intending to take their material up the Ottawa river to Ottawa, and thence by the canal down to Kingston. Between those two places a natural, though imperfect connection was already formed by a chain of minor lakes and small streams; the former rejoicing in such euphonious titles as Mud Lake, Sand Lake, and Dog Lake, and some of them measuring several miles in circuit. Accordingly, it only remained to cut through the intervening necks of land; so that although the so-called canal is more than a hundred miles in length, it possesses only a very few miles of cutting. It has long since been found to be almost useless,—and at the same time very expensive; for while so little actual cutting was required, still the number of locks and the amount of mason-work raised the cost of construction to more than a million sterling, which had to be borne by the British Government.

A gentleman narrates rather a singular anecdote of the Rideau Canal shortly after its completion. In 1832, while passing through in a pinnace from Kingston to Ottawa, he and his companions utterly lost their way! The notion of losing one's way on a canal would scarcely occur even to the most erratic and highly imaginative traveller; but such in this case was the fact. More extraordinary still, the contractor under whose management the canal had been made was of the party! Sailing across one of the little lakes, the voyagers were overtaken by night; and on gaining the place where they expected to find the outlet, no outlet was to be found. It was a clear starry October night; but the occupants of the pinnace were completely bewildered. A length of time was spent in fruitless rowing hither and thither, nothing being visible along the shore but an unbroken belt of close dark forest. At last, giving up their attempt in despair, the adventurers had resolved to camp in the woods till the morning; when one of the boatmen suddenly exclaimed—"Hark! what sound is that?" Resting on their oars, everyone strained an anxious ear, till a faint sound, as of water trickling over a rock, was heard. "We are all right now," cried the contractor, "that must be the water falling over the lock gates at the isthmus." And so it proved; the men bent to their oars, and in a short time the party were safely arrived at the cutting, laughing merrily over their dilemma.

During an evening spent with a Canadian friend, I gained his opinions as to the present standing of the country,—some of which it may not be amiss to subjoin.

"What do you think," I asked him, "of the present position and prospects of Canada?"

"You ask me a wide and rather complex question; for there is at once much good and much bad in our position."

"Suppose you begin, then, with the bad."

"Well, that lies on the side of our imports. You can see for yourself the deplorable state of our import trade; stagnation and insecurity are its prominent features."

"And whence do these mainly arise?"

"The stagnation springs from the want of money in the country; people can't afford to buy, therefore importers make but small sales. In order, however, to keep their connection together, the importers are forced to do some business; and finding it impossible to deal on safe and desirable terms, they grant long credits and bill renewals. Insecurity is the natural result."

"How long do you suppose this will last?"

"That no man can tell; still, it is fair to assume that with the improvement in America now beginning,—and with a better state of things in Britain, the import trade of the Dominion will commence to look up."

"And now, as to the more favourable prospect?"

"That, again, is all upon the side of our exports. The Dominion is rapidly coming to the front as a producing country."

"What, then, are the chief articles of produce?"

"The best way to answer that is to look at each province separately. Beginning at the sea-board, we have Nova Scotia and New Brunswick building and selling wooden ships, and working coal mines. Newfoundland is known over the world for its fisheries. Prince Edward Island builds ships; and exports oats and potatoes to Great Britain and the States. Quebec sends out square timber, and also builds ships."

"Shipbuilding would appear to be quite a large item."

"It is. Canada both builds and owns a great number of wooden vessels: indeed, she is said to have now the third carrying trade in the world."

"Is it possible! Britain, of course, stands first on that list; what country is second?"

"France stands next. But in calling Canada third, I speak with reference to ocean shipping alone; for if we take into account the number of vessels employed in the vast inland marine of the States, Canada ranks after the States."

"Well; to proceed with your *resumé* of the provinces."

"Advancing westwards from the sea-board, we have the great region of Ontario. Cereals, lumber, cattle, and minerals, are its chief products. In addition to its wheat, Ontario grows quantities of barley and peas, which find a ready market in the States."

"The States! Can the States not grow sufficient barley and peas for their own use?"

"Peas scarcely succeed across the frontier, on account of bugs,—which, for some mysterious cause, don't appear with us: and certain descriptions of Ontario barley cannot be equalled in the States for malting purposes."

"Ah! as a basis for American drinks!"

"Precisely. Then the Ontario farmers breed the best coarse wool sheep on the continent; a branch which shows great signs of future development. And Ontario possesses important mineral resources —iron, lead, antimony, and even a little gold; not to speak of phosphates. These, however, require capital to be brought forward."

"Canada, then, owes much to Ontario?"

"A very great deal. In the north-west, again, we have our new province of Manitoba, of which everybody has heard so much. I believe there is a great future in store for Manitoba, and that, when properly opened up and cultivated, this province will equal two or three American States put together in the production of grain."

"That, then, completes the list."

"Not quite—for we must not forget far away British Columbia. As yet British Columbia is only in its infancy; but it sends out no inconsiderable quantity of canned salmon, and is beginning to do something in lumber and coal, besides a little wool."

"Why, that is by no means a discouraging summary; showing that each of the provinces, upon its own merits, is doing fairly well."

"Each province shows a very pleasing result upon its export trade; but when the import business will pick up, no man can safely prophesy."

"Well, no doubt that will come with time. The Dominion, then, would seem to have a golden future in store."

"A golden future indeed,—if we can secure the two essentials, men and money. We want emigrants to settle on the new lands and work the soil; and we very greatly need men of capital to act along with them on a larger scale; and also to develop to the full those mineral resources which I have mentioned."

CHAPTER XVIII.

MONTREAL AND QUEBEC.

LEAVING the seat of Government one broiling morning, when all surrounding objects were quivering and shimmering in the sun-glare, I jogged down to Montreal by the Occidental Railway. The train consisted of an engine, guard's van, and a single carriage. In America, passengers who may have missed their connection sometimes take advantage of a goods train to reach their destination; in which case they are accommodated in the van, on payment of ordinary fare. Following the course of the Ottawa river, we arrived in the afternoon at Mile-End Station, Montreal, where I hired the remains of a cab, with a fossil horse, and drove to the Windsor Hotel. Montreal cabmen appear to regard the question of remuneration in a more unbiassed light than their *confrères* elsewhere, being willing—even eager—to conduct the passenger any reasonable distance for 25 cents., or 1s.

The Windsor Hotel is a masterpiece, at once as regards elegance and management, eclipsing even the best of the American houses. It is immense, and magnificent; while to the countless little conveniencies peculiar to American hotels it adds a British solidity, both in its furniture and in its table. The visitor revels in lofty saloons and vast colonnaded splendour for a daily charge of twelve shillings. Once in every week or fortnight the managers of the hotel clear the large supper-room for dancing, and request their guests not only to make use of it themselves, but to invite any city friends they may choose for the evening. The polished floor is very tempting, and hired musicians are provided by the proprietors. A number of Montreal residents appear at these miniature balls; and the privilege seems thoroughly appreciated. (The dances are conducted upon strict temperance principles,—*i.e.*, no one can obtain wine without paying for it).

The most striking features of Montreal are crooked streets, French inhabitants, Roman Catholic convents, and Dow's beer. This beverage is the best beer in Canada, and might vie with Bass. The original Dow is dead, but his memory remains green in the hearts of his grateful countrymen. Montreal streets are narrow and devious; and the city, while possessing as large a proportion of handsome buildings as other towns, has quite an old country aspect from its number of ancient houses, small squares, and tortuous alleys with no definite aim or termination.

The French element manifests itself both upon the shop sign-boards and in the broken *patois* which often greets the enquiring stranger, while the Church of Nôtre Dame, the unfinished Cathedral, and the prevalence of Roman Catholic monasteries and scholastic institutions supply further unmistakeable evidence. Until very recently, the lower French orders of Montreal lived in blind terror of the priests, never daring to be seen within a Protestant place of worship, nor to indulge in open friendship with their Protestant neighbours; till several of the more energetic Canadian clergy, deeming such a state of things to be a scandal to a Protestant country and the British flag, set themselves vigorously to combat the crushing domination of Mother Church. Some very exciting scenes marked the struggle; but the result now is that the Roman priesthood, though still preponderant, has greatly lost its temporal power.

Montreal possesses a monument of engineering skill in the Victoria Bridge, a railway viaduct across the St Lawrence, two miles long. This remarkable structure is of great strength—of which it had great need—having not only to resist the rapid river-current, but also to stand firm against the assaults of the floating ice masses which bear down upon it in winter.

In point of situation, Montreal is highly favoured. Behind it rises "The Mountain," a long, low ridge covered with trees, which, if not beautiful in itself, yet affords a fine vantage ground for a view. The city is built on an island of its own name, lying at the junction of the great streams St Lawrence and Ottawa; but its insulated position becomes apparent to the spectator only when surveyed from the commanding eminence.

The slopes of the Mountain have been selected by wealthy citizens for building sites; and numerous handsome villas—some castellated, others plain—are perched upon the steep. These residences are approached by toilsome ascents leading straight up the face of the hill; which, when covered with snow, present great attractions for toboggining. On a winter's afternoon the toboggins may be seen shooting down these inclines in untiring streams, giving rise to a variety of *contretemps*, both comic and serious. When the snow has been beaten into a hard track almost resembling ice, the velocity of the descent is tremendous, and the most skilful guidance is required to prevent catastrophe. The hill roads at their lower termination meet the public highway at a direct right angle, so that on reaching the foot of the declivity the toboggins have to be turned sharply round into the main road, along the level surface of which they skim by their acquired impetus for a long way. Vehicles are constantly passing and repassing on the highway, but the tobogginers pursue their pastime with a fine disregard of contingencies, contentedly accepting the chances of collision with any suddenly approaching cart or sleigh. Occasionally some one is killed, which gives the amusement a little additional excitement, and very often some one is hurt, which also helps to relieve the monotony.

An incident which lately occurred may not be uninteresting, as at once laughable and authentic. Down one of the steep roads, on a frosty day, the toboggins were pouring in ceaseless succession, when a little boy, posted about half-way down the hill, stepped out into the middle of the road to gaze after a toboggin which had just shot past. While his attention was thus engaged, another toboggin rushed rapidly down on him. Its occupants shouted to him to get out of the way; but his boyish eyes were enviously fixed upon the first toboggin, and his boyish ears were deaf to warning; so the second sled, sweeping down upon his fat little calves, carried his legs clean from under him, and shot him straight up into the air. Describing a complete somersault, he landed on his feet on the very spot where he had been standing,—wondering vastly, but uninjured;

while the guilty toboggin was by this time forty yards below, pursuing its resistless descent.

After some stay in Montreal, during which I was again much indebted to Canadian hospitality, I went on board the steamer one evening to proceed down the St Lawrence to Quebec. The distance between the two places is a hundred and eighty miles, which the steamers "Quebec" and "Montreal," of the Richelieu and Ontario line, accomplish in twelve hours. A substantial supper disposed of, I was seated on the deck rapt in moonlight and meditation, when a very unwonted sound broke the evening calm. It can never be! And yet,—is it possible! Hark! now it swells out on the still night air with a weird and piercing shrillness; now it sinks again in the distance, with a mournful, gruesome cadence. Can my patriotic ear be mistaken? No; there it is, beyond the shadow of a doubt, in all its native vigour, as if summoning a thousand clans over the breezy Scottish heather, my country's harp—the BAGPIPES! Starting to my feet, I make for the bows of the vessel, whence the strain seems to proceed; and lo! there in a corner stand four Caledonians, grandly patriotic from the combined influence of their national instrument and a large bottle of their own mountain-dew. The piper strikes up a lively strathspey; and there go my Celtic wights—hands up—toes and heels flying madly—figure eight, in and out—set to partners—quick reel time—faster and faster—till they finish with a " Hooch!" that makes the old boat ring from stem to stern! And a Yankee standing by, surprised for a moment out of his native " wonder-at-nothing," remarks in an awe-struck tone, that " Snakes is simply nothin' to it,—*con*sarn him, anyhow!"

The piper and his comrades proved to be Scotch masons, going down to Quebec in the prospect of a job.

Awaking at seven o'clock the next morning, I found the steamer moored to the quay at Quebec, and lost no time in going on shore. Becoming hopelessly involved amid a chaos of French cabmen, I was timeously rescued by the driver of the Russell House omnibus, who bore me to his vehicle shouting back triumph and contempt at his baffled opponents. Then ascending a precipitous street, we wound in and out through a labyrinth, till my charioteer, with a precision that seemed truly marvellous, emerged right in front of the hotel. Transatlantic politeness compels the driver of an omnibus to back his conveyance against the pavement; so that the occupants in alighting step directly upon the flags, instead of into the mud-heap which fringes the British side-walk. The Russell House, Quebec, being the third or fourth establishment of that name which I had met with in my travels, the enquiry naturally suggested itself—Who was Russell? Was he a prince of hotel speculators, or an eminent statesman, or a hero, or a myth? All my efforts to obtain light upon this curiously interesting question proved futile; and it remains yet unsolved.

Quebec is two-thirds French—and wholly old-fashioned. The streets are narrow and hilly, the paving is bad, and the city possesses an aristocracy. In Quebec "position is everything," (as old Lillywhite was wont to remark when taking guard); the old families form a distinct and exclusive set, and view with scorn the *nouveau riche*. The lower orders of the French are lazy and inert,—though the working classes generally are seldom unwilling to engage in riot and disaffection. A labour strike in Quebec means sticks and stones and street rows; and while my own experience of the city did not include such a display of popular feeling, a very creditable example occurred shortly after my departure.

Quebec boasts more sights of interest than any other Canadian town, both from its natural scenery and historical associations,—a fact fully recognised by its hack-drivers. Cab-stands are ubiquitous, and every cab-stand owns twenty pairs of hawk eyes, twenty elevated and persuasive fingers, and twenty clamouring voices. In no place was I so incessantly importuned; every stranger is regarded as a sightseer, and every sightseer is lawful prey. The only individual whom I can think of as at all likely to overawe a horde of Quebec hackmen is the " Unprotected British Female Abroad." That redoubtable personage, with one single glare from behind her coloured spectacles, and one winning flourish of her umbrella, would, I am morally certain, be enough to scatter even the most undaunted. The majority of the men are French Canadians; and their running broadside, delivered in broken English, is something like this—

Huge fiend with a black beard, imperiously; " Dis way, I say,—jomp in!"

Small man with a squeaky treble; " Falls of Montmorenci, m'sieu, tree dollar!"

Being devoid both of cleanliness and grammar,—"Here you is, sir; take you ver' much cheap indeed!"

Powerful voice, "Waggon, sir? Best in de city!"

Seductive party, affectionately; " Hack, sir! Drive you all round de city for one dollar?"

With the intention of visiting the Falls of Montmorenci, I directed the hotel porter to find me the vehicle with the least truculent driver; and prepared to set out. From the four corners of the cab rose upright poles on which an awning was stretched, the front, back, and sides being left entirely open. This style of machine is very suitable for hot weather, as the covered top protects the inmate from the sun, while the absence of sides provides for fresh air. The driver was a French Canadian with a tolerable knowledge of English, and the proffer of a cigar opened up the flow of his information to the full. Descending several steep streets, we reached the banks of the Charles River, on the banks of which I saw a number of shipbuilding yards. My cabman informed me that the trade was then in a pretty active state. A mile or so beyond the city we passed close to a large building among some trees.

"Dat," said my cicerone, "will be de lunatic asylum. It is in quite flourishing state just now—great number of lunatics."

Shortly afterwards (in true "guide-book" style); "Dis leetle village will be Beauport; and dere, (pointing with his whip to a tumble down edifice with the dimensions of a stable and the unsightliness of a board-school), dese are de ruins of Montcalm's old house. De great Général Montcalm, you onderstand."

"Why, there is a sad want of romance about those ruins! In fact, they are the feeblest ruins I ever saw. Montcalm can't have been ambitious in his choice of a residence."

"Ah, oui! Montcalm was ver' great général, ver' great man, *certainement!*"

"I have no doubt of it; but the ruins are not up to the mark. You have never been in the old country, I suppose?"

"Across de ocean?" No, sare."

"That accounts for your enthusiasm. Now if you went to England, you would have an opportunity of cultivating a really appreciative taste for ruins."

"Ah oui, oui! Den you have de grand ruins in England, sare?"

"Unrivalled. In the matter of really effective ruins we defy competition."

"Tonnerre! Is dat so?"

Halting a little farther on,—

"From dis place you will look back and observe de magnifique tableau of de city and Point Levi. De stranger will say Quebec to be de most beautiful city of Canada. And now we approach de Falls."

Arrived in the vicinity of the Falls, we stopped before a little inn, to the interior of which the driver directed me for a guide, while he proceeded to stable his horse. The landlady's command of English was as bad as her beer,—which, to use a Canadian expression, "would kill at a hundred yards." (From the distantly destructive power attributed to a certain low grade of Dominion whisky, the liquor in question is familiarly known as "forty-rod whisky.") Procuring a guide, and paying an entrance fee, I was admitted within the enclosure of the Falls, and gave myself up for some time to the enjoyment of a truly magnificent sight. The Falls of Montmorenci are considerably higher than those of Niagara— though of infinitely less volume; but the latter feature increases rather than detracts from their effect. At Niagara all is water, and that in a very broad body; at Montmorenci the river leaps through a confined gorge, and the narrowness of the fall impresses the beholder with a grander idea of height; while the great perpendicular cliffs crowned with tall pines and stretching back from either side, impart a telling variety to the scene.

Next day, securing the services of the same cabman, I drove out upon the Plains of Abraham, from the edge of which there is a commanding view of the river. (On my making inquiry of my conductor as to the history of Abraham, he definitely established the identity of that personage with the patriarch.) Wolfe's monument, which stands upon the Plains a short distance outside of the town, is an insult to Wolfe and a disgrace to the British nation, being, from its diminutive size and meagre appearance, better fitted for a country churchyard than a position of publicity.

Quebec is thickly walled and strongly fortified, its citadel being almost impregnable. Some assert that the citadel is the strongest in existence next to Gibraltar. Immediately beneath the fortress a broad esplanade is in course of construction, which, hanging as it were on the very side of the cliff, looks sheer down upon the wharves and the lower town. A fine view of the country for leagues surrounding is obtained from the esplanade; and the undulating land, rolling up in the distance to encircling chains of mountain, is very suggestive of a Stirlingshire valley bounded by the Ochils. Quebec is a place in which the stranger may spend a length of time with interest:—but we must hasten on to Boston.

CHAPTER XIX.

THE LEARNED CITY.

THE States once more! It was the witching hour of dinner, and I was ensconced at the table d'hote of the Revere House, Boston. Suddenly a stentorian voice at my side exclaimed—

"Waiter! I'll take chowder soup, fried whitefish, mutton cutlet—hm!—and broiled quail and plain lobster,—with potatoes, fried parsnips, succotash and stewed tomatoes."

I looked up.

"And stay, waiter; I guess you may bring me some calf's head—and a turkey wing and a sausage—and chicken salad and hominy. Yes,—that's all."

Americans are fond of mixtures; but this was something beyond the common. I recognised at once that my neighbour was no ordinary man. Presently, perceiving by his delicate national intuition that I was a foreigner, he observed graciously—

"Been long over, sir?"

"Why, about six months."

"Is that so? Travelling around, I guess?"

"Well, I have gone over a good deal of country, first and last."

"Ah! Been across California way, sir? That is my place, down to Sacramento City."

"I am sorry to say I didn't manage to go so far."

"That's a pity, now; for it is really a handsome spot. Well, I and my wife are on a trip like yourself; we have plenty of time and nothing to occupy us. My wife took sick this afternoon and stopped out from dinner,—I'm sorry she's not here, for I should have liked to introduce you. She is quite fond of meeting strangers."

(I expressed my keen sense of desolation at the absence of the fair sufferer.)

"Well sir, I purchased real estate in my district some years ago; property rose, and I realised a pile. Then I quitted business."

"Indeed? There has been a vast amount of speculation in Californian land, from all accounts."

"There has, sir;—but I can tell you that every man who invests don't come out so well as I did,—for I went in on the rise, and sold out on top figures. The proceeds of my property gave me an income of twenty thousand dollars; so now I and my wife spend our time travelling over the world to gain information. Wonderful thing travelling to *ex*pand the mind, sir."

"I agree with you there—most entirely!"

"We have been to quite a number of places since we commenced—Britain, France, Russia, Egypt, *and* Asia Minor; and I always took care to learn something as I went along. I made it a point to know the facts of each *lo*cality."

"Why, you must have picked up no end of information at that rate!"

"Well yes, I consider that I have. What a shocking state, now, the *fi*nances of Egypt are in at present! I posted myself carefully on that subject when I was in the country. Have you studied the question, sir?"

"I'm extremely sorry I have not."

"Ah, then I guess I needn't enter upon it. It is interesting, too, to know the ancient history of those countries, sir. We were fond of going about the Pyramids, and looking back to Marcus Anthony and Cleoppatra."

"It must have been a singularly fascinating retrospect!"

"I often think what queer ideas of life these ancient parties must have had. I guess, now, if you could raise them out of their mummies and plant them down in Fifth Avenue, New York City, they would see some things that would surprise them!"

"I don't doubt that for one moment."

"They would naturally feel kind of vexed at first, to find we had gone ahead of them; but they would begin to be pleased, I know, when they saw the Elevated Railroad and the New Post Office."

"I am sure they would. Those evidences of progress would be likely to yield them a very rare satisfaction."

"And they would be quite gratified with Tony Pastor's the*ay*ter and Niblo's Garden. They were wonderful chaps in these old times for the*ay*ters and circuses; it shows they had a mighty cute notion of how to spend their evenings."

"They did know a thing or two, certainly."

"You may bet your bottom dollar on that! Take the ancient Greeks now;—why, they can whip us even yet in statuary and carving! They had an elegant notion of working in stone, sir."

"Inimitable. I suppose you have visited Greece?"

"We ran through the country two summers ago."

"You would find there any amount of material for research?"

"*Im*mense, sir. We used to go around the ruins in the day-time, and *per*use the ancient history in the evenings."

"Why, that was a capital plan. I should say you

could hardly fail to gain a very thorough acquaintance with the relics of the past in that way."

"Yes, I guess it was a happy idea. I liked to read about those Pattollemies, the former rulers of Greece."

"Dear me! I remember poring over those beggars as a schoolboy with a very painful interest."

"And then Hannibal—and Leonidas and the Spartans—and the rest of them. What a beautiful simplicity there was in ancient Greek life,—wasn't there, now!" "(Waiter!)"

"Yes, sir."

"Squash pie, charlotte russe, apple fritters, and ice cream and coffee.)"

"—Yes, sir, a most *be*-autiful simplicity. Do you know, now, Leonidas and Thermollypæ quite reminded me of the siege of Vicksburg?"

"Ah! you were in the war, then, I suppose?"

"I was, sir;—through the whole fight."

"Then you would go over the classic soil of Greece quite as a military critic."

"Why yes; I couldn't help saying to myself at times,—'If Ulysses S. Grant, or Phil Sheridan, had been there, instead of Xerxes or the other chap, they would have acted quite differently.'"

"Well," said I, rising to go,—" it has been a great

pleasure to me to have met you; and I am glad to have interchanged our thoughts on these old familiar themes."

"So am I, sir; *ve*ry pleased indeed. Are you going back to Britain soon, may I *in*quire?"

" In about a fortnight, I think."

"We mean taking a run through Denmark and Sweden this fall, and we might perhaps see you passing through Britain."

"Delighted, sir, I am sure." So we exchanged cards, and parted.

Boston is exceedingly old world, more so than any city I saw. (I noticed several unmistakeable cases of inebriation,—which were particularly home-like.) The city is the seat of Columbian learning and literature, and the resort of blue-stockings. In Boston the American Eagle, that proud and noble fowl, passing for the nonce from the consideration of the absorbing commercial problem, applies himself to the differential calculus and the *pons asinorum*. In New York, when a new comer seeks admittance into society, the question asked is, "How much have you got?" but in Boston it becomes, "How much do you know?" Great is the influence of learning! Even the waiter who ministered to my wants had an abnormally large forehead, and wore a more sepulchrally impassive expression than most of his kind. He was a Memnon, a Sphinx,—almost a Beaconsfield!

The cultivation of knowledge is greatly aided in Boston by the presence of Harvard University; which, though situated in the suburb of New Cambridge, may yet claim to belong to the city. The University consists of a cluster of red brick buildings, surrounded by fine trees. As I strolled through the quadrangles and contemplated the students, I thought that the latter presented a not un-English appearance, in their leaning towards plaid suits, athletics, and the use of slang. While I gazed upon the august pile, my reverie was interrupted by a nasal voice—

"*Ad*miring our University, Sir?"

"Yes," I said, "I am. It looks very pleasant, if not venerable as yet; but antiquity will come with time."

"Quite true, sir. So will rats." And the owner of the voice passed on.

Boston is the head-quarters of the national game of baseball; and I witnessed a championship match between nine of Boston and nine of Chicago, in which the capital of the West prevailed. The enclosure was thronged with rapt and highly appreciative spectators, who loudly applauded the fine bits of play. The contestants were all professionals—most of them quite young; and their fielding and catching were extraordinary, the ball being returned from any distance straight to the desired spot like a flash of lightning. The skill and activity of these baseball players would almost put to shame an all-England eleven. They are handsomely remunerated by the gate receipts, each man making from £150 to £500 annually.

It was in Boston first that my attention was drawn to the American dust wrapper. This is a whitey-brown linen vestment reaching from the neck to the feet, and common to both sexes. With ladies it is passable—at times even elegant; but the sterner sex thus attired give one the unhappy idea of elongated journeymen painters. Outside of New York, the male Yankee's taste in dress is conspicuous by its absence. There are two prominent classes, the one representing capital, the other fashion. The former class wear black clothes, of no special cut or shape, Wellington boots—frequently displayed by a brevity of trouser, and wide-awake hats of varied hues. The *tout ensemble* suggests a respectable (and rather oily) grocer,—in somebody else's clothes. The fashionables, again, spoil an otherwise tolerable costume by a tendency to run to collar and wrist-cuffs, and huge cat's-eye rings and breast-pins.

The time drawing near when I should again ascend

the deck of the ocean steamship, I left Boston for New York one evening, *via* Fall River. A short railway journey brought me to Fall River wharf, where the steamer was lying: and there a point in the American character strikingly manifested itself. There was an immense crowd of passengers, many of whom had not engaged berths beforehand, and who were therefore obliged to apply for them at the purser's office on board the steamer. These persons quietly fell into a long line in the most orderly way, and waited their turn with perfect patience. The component parts of a British assemblage on such an occasion would throng upon each other pell mell, elbowing and treading, with diffusive and impartial bad language, The American method appears preferable; and yet—America is a Republic!

The steamer, "The Bristol," of the Old Colony line, was a *fac-simile*, only on a larger scale, of the St Lawrence boats—a white towering immensity, with three tiers of saloons, and a forest of funnels or "smoke-stacks." The Americans claim for their river steamers the title of "floating palaces;" nor is it misapplied. The "Bristol," one of the most famous of those grand craft, is nearly four hundred feet long by fifty beam, while at the paddle-box wings the deck so greatly overhangs the sides, that the breadth is eighty feet. Her paddle-wheels are thirty-eight feet in diameter, and her funnels fifty feet high. She has five hundred double-berthed state-rooms; while fully as many more passengers can be accommodated on mattresses on the saloon floor. She enjoys an immunity from fleas. On the inside of each state-room door are hung two cork life-jackets, —affording to its inmates a mingled sense of security and its opposite. The saloons extend the whole length of the boat, and are conspicuous for gilding, costly furniture, and ornamented columns; while the supper cabin resembles the hall of a hotel. The whole ship is lighted by gas. She draws eleven feet of water, and attains a speed of seventeen miles an hour; for while apparently cumbrous by her vast superstructure, she has fine lines below. On the passage between Fall River and New York, the open Atlantic has to be encountered for more than an hour, and a heavy swell sometimes runs up Long Island Sound; but the "Bristol" is an admirable sea boat, and as stiff as a Presbyterian Church. The charge for the journey, inclusive of railway fare from Boston—though not of meals and private stateroom —is only a dollar and a half.

By daylight on the following morning we were sailing up amidst the pretty river scenery of the Hudson, and by eight o'clock we found ourselves alongside of the quay at New York.

CHAPTER XX.

EASTWARDS AWAY.

New York in summer is very different from New York in winter. The heat is excessive, and its effects are everywhere visible. Sun-blinds decorate the shops; sundry of the population affect linen coats and ditto nether garments; while hairdressers and shampooists drive a lively trade. There is in New York a fashionable summer "crop," for purposes of coolness, by which the cranium is almost denuded of its covering. Many of the hotel barbers are born (and go through life) without a vestige of conscience; one operator, after abbreviating my hair so as to make me the object of criminal suspicion for months to come, had the unblushing effrontery to demand a dollar in payment!

When the mercury indicates ninety or a hundred in the shade, life ceases to be worth living. Those who are not called by business to active exertion sit in the hotel with their vests thrown open, and their feet (not uncommonly) projected out of the window; while such unfortunates as are compelled to be astir drag themselves wearily along the shady side of the street, and drip continuously. Physically and morally, one is reduced to a pulp; it is too hot to eat, too hot to sleep,—too hot even to think. The sole question upon which the mind can rest with pleasure, is the retrospect of the last cooling drink, or the prospect of the next one. The negro waiter is the only individual who seems to have any remaining satisfaction in existence. That coal-black functionary smiles and perspires, and perspires and smiles, and trots hither and thither bringing "cobblers" and ice creams, with an expression of composure that is ineffable. Fans are used in the churches on Sunday, without distinction of sex. Street-hawkers respond to the wants of the humbler population with stalls of bananas, sliced pine-apples, and peanuts. The first two are peculiar to the summer months; but the peanut is perennial and ubiquitous, —forming indeed a main element in the American Constitution. Without peanuts, America would cease to be America. Produced chiefly in Virginia, and distributed throughout the States, peanuts are roasted like chestnuts and vended everywhere; being in as universal demand as the all-pervading orange so dear to the heart of the British cad.

The various small enclosures and public gardens interspersed among the streets of New York appear like oases in the warm weather, by the rich verdure of their grass and the umbrage of their trees. Some of the houses in the better portion of the city have their walls clad with thickly-growing creepers, which cling to the dull red stone like masses of clustering ivy. Central Park, with all its vegetation in full luxuriance, appears to great advantage; while its shaded alleys become the favourite retreats of children, nurses, and goat-carriages. New Yorkers very often entrust their little ones to the care of French *bonnes*, so that the children learn to speak French fluently.

Staten and Coney Islands, lying some distance down the harbour, are much sought in summer by hot and dusty citizens; who either own private seaside residences, or else take up their quarters in the mammoth marine hotels.

At last, one burning June morning, I bade farewell to Columbia, and embarked with seventy or eighty fellow-passengers on board the steamer. *Apropos* of our start, rather a good story is told of the departure of a Cunard ship from the Jersey City dock. The vessel was backing slowly out from her berth into the stream, her decks thronged with passengers interchanging adieux and repartee with the concourse of spectators on the quay. Suddenly, as is often the case at a social gathering, a solemn hush came over both assemblages, so that the faintest sound might have been heard. Then from the midst of the crowd upon the quay rose a shrill Western voice calling to the receding steamer—

"Jest like you slow-goin' Britishers—always do everythin' starn first!"

A great roar of laughter, echoing and re-echoing till the ship had reached midchannel, put to flight the silence.

Our passage home was very pleasant. We fraternized and formed cliques, joked and played cards; while the lady portion of the community found ample occupation in the discussion of their neighbours, and the fabrication of mild scandal. We had several couples on board (of opposite sex), who found a strange attraction in the contemplation of the waste of waters from the back of the wheel-house (a very retired spot), and who were always much confused by the appearance of any third party. Unluckily, the space behind the wheel-house was too limited to accommodate more than one pair at a time, and those who first secured it generally remained for a lengthened period; so that the less fortunate couples were doomed to disappointment and publicity. There were several rude and unfeeling passengers, who—emanating chiefly from the smoking-room—sustained an organised espionage over such amatory proceedings, and were wont to break in upon the fond couples when in the blissful act of embracing the opportunity—and each other. But such conduct can be viewed by every right-minded person only with reprobation.

On the morning of the eleventh day the steamer dropped anchor at Greenock; and landing from the tender, I found myself once more on the soil of old Scotland.

APPENDIX.

FIFTH AVENUE HOTEL, N. Y.
DARLING, GRISWOLD, & CO.

BREAKFAST.

BROILED.

Beefsteak.	Tripe, plain.	Pickled Tripe.	Veal Cutlets.
Calf's Liver.	Smoked Bacon.	Mutton Chops.	Chicken.
Mutton Kidneys.	Pig's Feet breaded.	Ham.	Lamb Chops.
	Pork Chops.		

FRIED.

Pig's Feet breaded.	Oysters with crumbs.	Pickled Tripe.
Calf's Liver.	Sausages.	Clams.
	Pork Chops.	

STEWED.

Clams.	Veal and Mutton Kidneys.	Oysters.
	Hashed Meat.	

FISH.

Fried Codfish, with pork.	Salt Codfish, with cream.	Hashed Fish.
Broiled Salt Mackerel.	Smoked Salmon.	Digby Herrings.
Broiled Bluefish.		Fish Balls.
Fried Panfish.		Fried Smelts.

EGGS.

Omelets, plain, or with parsley, onions, ham, kidneys, or cheese, boiled, fried, scrambled, or dropped.

COLD MEATS.

Roast Beef.	Corned Beef.	Tongue.	Ham.

POTATOES.

Stewed.	Lyonnaise.	Fried.	Baked.

Fried Indian Pudding.	Oatmeal Mush.	Dry and Dipped Toast.
Boston Brown Bread.	Muffins.	Rice Cakes.
Graham Bread.	Graham Rolls.	Cracked Wheat.
Corn Bread.	French Rolls.	Hominy.
Fried Hominy.	English Muffins.	Buckwheat Cakes.

Coffee, Chocolate, Oolong, Green and English Breakfast Tea.

BREAKFAST, from 7 to 11.   LUNCH, from 1 to 2.
     DINNER, from 2 to 5, and at 5½ precisely, table d'hôte.
TEA, from 6 to 9.   SUPPER, from 9 to 12.
     DINNER ON SUNDAYS, 2 and 5½.   BREAKFAST, 8.

HOURS FOR CHILDREN AND SERVANTS.

BREAKFAST, 7.   DINNER, 1.   TEA, 6.

No Reserved Seats at Breakfast.

DINNER.

Oysters on half shell.

SOUPS.
Ox Joint.   Fish Chowder.

FISH.
Boiled Sheepshead, Hollandaise sauce.   Broiled Whitefish, parsley sauce.

BOILED.
Leg of Mutton, caper sauce.   Corned Beef and cabbage
Chicken and pork.   Calf's Head, brain sauce.
Beef Tongue.   Ham.

COLD DISHES.
Beef Tongues.   à la mode Beef.   Roast Beef.   Boned Turkey.
Chicken Salad.   Lobster plain.   Ham.   Lobster Salad.

ENTREES.
Salmi of Grouse with jelly.
Turkey Wings braisés with green peas.
Codfish fried, English Style.
Oysters à la Poulette
Mutton Cutlets, sauce piquante.
Sausages with Brussels sprouts.
Broiled Quail on toast.

ROAST.
Chicken.   Ham, champagne sauce.   Mongrel Duck.
Beef.   Lamb, mint sauce.   Turkey.

GAME.
Venison.

VEGETABLES.
Boiled Potatoes.   Stewed Tomatoes.   Onions
Mashed Potatoes.   Beets.   Turnips.   Succotash.
Hominy.   Spinach.   Fried Parsnips.
Sweet Potatoes.   Cauliflower.

PASTRY.
Bread pudding, brandy sauce.
Rice pudding.   Squash pie.
Raspberry puffs   Mince pie
Charlotte russe.   Currant cake.
Ginger snaps.

DESSERT.
Figs.   Grapes.   Pears.   Oranges.   Apples.
English Walnuts.   Almonds.   Pecan Nuts.   Raisins.
Lemon Ice Cream.   Mosel Sherbet.
Coffee.

APPENDIX. 293

WINE LIST.
CHAMPAGNE.

Möet & Chandon Extra Dry Cabinet	Pts. $1 75	Qts.	$3 50
Giesler & Co., Dry Sillery	„ 1 50	„	3 00
G. H. Mumm & Co's Dry Verzenay	„ 1 50	„	3 00
G. H. Mumm & Co's Extra Dry Verzenay	„ 1 75	„	3 50
G. H. Mumm, Cordon Rouge	„ 1 75	„	3 50
Piper Heidsieck	„ 1 50	„	3 00
Schreider, N. H., Dry	„ 1 50	„	3 00
Krug & Co.	„ 1 50	„	3 00
Delmonico half pints $1 00	„ 1 75	„	3 50
L. Roederer's Dry Sillery	„ 1 75	„	3 50
L. Roederer's Carte Blanche	„ 1 75	„	3 50
Dry Monopole	„ 1 75	„	3 50
Giesler & Co., Superior Extra Dry	„ 1 75	„	3 50
Moet & Chandon, Imperial Green Seal	„ 1 75	„	3 50
Ve Clicquot, Ponsardin	„ 1 75	„	3 50
Pommery Sec	„ 1 75	„	3 50

AMERICAN SPARKLING WINES.

California Eclipse, Extra Dry	Pts. $1 00	Qts.	$2 80
Werk's Catawba, Golden Eagle	„ 1 00	„	2 00
Werk's Golden Eagle, Dry		„	2 00
American Wine Co's Imperial	„ 1 00	„	2 00
Urbana Wine Co., Gold Seal	„ 1 00	„	2 00

AMERICAN STILL WINES.

California Claret	Pts. $0 50	Qts.	$1 00
Angelica, Los Angelos Vintage	„ 75	„	1 50
Muscatel	„ 75	„	1 50
California Port	„ 75	„	1 50
California Hock	„ 75	„	1 50
American Wine Co., Concord		„	1 50
Werk's Dry Catawba, 1870	Pts. 75	„	1 50
Kelley's Island Dry Catawba	„ 50	„	1 00
Currant		„	1 50

SHERRY.

Table Pale, Dry	Pts. $1 00	Qts.	$1 50
Brown	,, 1 25	,,	2 00
Pale Light Wine	,, 1 25	,,	2 00
Y. Pale D. Yriartes, delicate			2 50
Vino de Pasto, Pale, Dry Wine			2 50
Three Grapes, Ysasi & Co			3 00
Gastelus' Old Pale, rich but delicate			3 00
Ysasi & Co's Imperial			3 00
Amontillado, Ysasi & Co.			3 00
Topaz Sherry, very pale			2 50
S. S., full flavour			4 00
Queen's, Ysasi & Co			4 00
Duartes' V. V. S. Dry Wine			5 00
Stevens' Sherry, old and soft			6 00
Ashburton, Amontillado, very dry			6 00

MADEIRA.

Monteiro, M. T.	$2 50
Leacock's O. L. P.	5 00
Sir John Keene	6 50
Monteiro Meteor, J. W. Boot	6 50
West India, Rapid	7 50
Welch's Old Family	8 00
East India	9 00
N. G. & M. £100, 1818	10 00
Com. Rodgers' Private Stock	10 00
Curious Old Pale Madeira, selected by J. D. & M. Williams, from Maris' gift wine	10 00
Israel Thorndike's Sercial	14 00
Gibb's Old Pale Newport, 70 years old	15 00

PORT.

Sandeman's Oporto	$2 00
Sandeman's Old Port	3 00
White Port, very old	4 00
Cockburn's Old Port	5 00

CLARET.

CRUSE AND FILS FRERES.

Médoc	Pts. $0 40	Qts.	$0 75
Château Bouliac	„ 50	„	1 00
St Julien	„ 75	„	1 50
St Julien, Superior	„ 1 00	„	2 00
Margaux	„ 1 00	„	2 00
Larose	„ 1 25	„	2 50
Léoville	„ 1 25	„	2 50
Grand Vin Pontet Canet, 1865	„ 1 25	„	2 50
Latour	„ 1 75	„	3 50
Lafite	„ 2 25	„	4 50
Grand Vin Château Leoville, 1865			5 00
„ „ Lafite, 1865			6 00
„ „ Margaux, 1847			7 00

BRANDENBURG FRERES.

Château Larose	Pts. $1 25	Qts.	$2 50

BARTON AND GUESTIER.

Floirac	Pts. $0 75	Qts.	$1 50
St Julien, 1874	„ 1 00	„	2 00

BURGUNDY.

Sparkling St Peray		Qts.	$3 50
Beaune	Pts. $1 25	„	2 50
Nuits	„ 2 00	„	3 50
Chambertin	„ 2 00	„	4 00
Romanée Conti	„ 2 50	„	5 00
Clos de Vougeot	„ 3 00	„	6 00

SAUTERNES.

Sauternes	Pts. $0 75	Qts.	$1 50
Haut Sauternes	„ 1 00	„	2 00
Latour Blanche, sweet	„ 1 25	„	2 50
Chablis	„ 1 50	„	3 00
Château Yquem	„ 2 00	„	4 00

ITALIAN WINES.

Monbazillac	Qts.	$3 00

HOCK.

D. LEIDEN AND HENKEL AND CO.

Niersteiner	Pts. $0 75	Qts. $1 50
Laubenheimer	„ 0 75	„ 1 50
Hochheimer	„ 1 00	„ 2 00
Sparkling Hock	„ 1 50	„ 3 00
Marcobrunner, delicate		3 00
Rudesheimer Berg		4 00
Johannisberg, Green Seal (D. Leiden & Co.)		5 00
„ Silver Bronze Seal „		6 00
Steinberger Cabinet, 1862 . „		6 00
Johannisberg, Gold Seal, 1862 . „		8 00

MOSEL.

HENKEL AND CO.

Sparkling Muscatel	Pts. $1 50	Qts. $3 00
Ausbruch, still and dry		4 00

BRANDIES.

IMPORTED BY PARAN STEVENS.

Otard, Dupuy, & Co.	$3 50
„ „ 1836	5 00
„ „ 1800	6 50

ALE AND PORTER.

Robert Younger's Edinburgh Ale	Pts. $0 35	
Bass & Co.'s	„ 35	
Bass & Co.'s (white label)	„ 35	
London Porter	„ 35	
Guiness's Dublin Porter	„ 35	
Smithwick's Kilkenny Porter	Pts. $0 35	Qts. 65
Crab Apple Cider	„ 35	„ 70
Tivoli Berlin Beer	35	
Lager Beer	20	
Bass & Co.'s Ales, on draught	20	

LIQUEURS, CORDIALS, ETC.

Kümmel, Chartreuse, Curaçao, Maraschino, Anisette, Kirschwasser, Vermouth, Absinthe, Bénédictine, etc.

CORKAGE $1.00 PER BOTTLE.

Each Waiter is provided with wine card and pencil.

Griffith & Farran

A SELECT LIST

of Some of the Most POPULAR BOOKS

Published and Sold by

GRIFFITH & FARRAN

Including

- EDUCATIONAL BOOKS
- BOOKS FOR CHILDREN
- DEVOTIONAL BOOKS
- HOLY BIBLES, COMMON PRAYERS, &c.

Suitable for School Prizes, Birthday and Confirmation Gifts, &c., &c.

Complete Catalogues post free upon application.

ST. PAUL'S CHURCHYARD, LONDON.

Books for Children.

Arranged according to Prices.

Ten Shillings and Sixpence, cloth elegant.

Child Life in Japan and Japanese Child Stories.
By M. CHAPLIN AYRTON. With Seven full-page Illustrations, drawn and engraved by Japanese artists, and many smaller ones. Quarto, cloth elegant.

Seven Shillings and Sixpence each, cloth elegant.

The Looking-Glass for the Mind. Cuts by BEWICK.

The Young Buglers:
A Tale of the Peninsular War. By G. A. HENTY, Author of "Out on the Pampas," &c. With Eight full-page pictures and numerous plans of Battles.

Six Shillings each, cloth elegant, with Illustrations.

Flyaway Fairies and Baby Blossoms. Paper boards.
By L. CLARKSON.

Golden Threads from an Ancient Loom;
Das Nibelungenlied adapted to the use of Young Readers. By LYDIA HANDS. Dedicated by permission to Thomas Carlyle. With Fourteen Wood Engravings by J. SCHNORR, of Carolsfeld. Royal 4to.

Kingston's (W. H. G.) Will Weatherhelm.
„ *The Missing Ship.*
„ *The Three Admirals.*
„ *True Blue.*
„ *Paddy Finn.*
„ *Three Midshipmen.*
„ *Three Lieutenants.*
„ *Three Commanders.*
„ *Hurricane Hurry.*
„ *Won from the Waves.*

Little Loving Heart's Poem Book. By M. E. TUPPER. 40 Illustrations.

Middy and Ensign; Or, The Jungle Station. By G. MANVILLE FENN.

Any Book sent Post Free upon receipt of Stamps to value of Published Price. A Liberal Discount to the Clergy and the Scholastic Profession.

St Paul's Churchyard, London. 3

Five Shillings each, cloth elegant.

Illustrated by eminent Artists.

Belton Scholarship, The.
By BERNARD HELDMANN.

Gentleman Cadet (The):
By Lieut.-Colonel DRAYSON.

Hair-Breadth Escapes;
Or, The Adventures of Three Boys in South Africa. By the Rev. H. C. ADAMS.

Holly Berries.
By AMY E. BLANCHARD. Coloured Illustrations by Ida Waugh. Paper boards.

In Times of Peril.
By G. A. HENTY.

Kingston's Rival Crusoes (The).
(Or bevelled boards, gilt edges, 6s.)

Wee Babies.
Illustrated by IDA WAUGH. Paper boards.

Who did it?
By the Rev. H. C. ADAMS.

Favourite Picture Book (The) and Nursery Companion.
⁎ This may also be had in four parts, in paper boards, fancy wrapper, price 1s. each, or coloured Illustrations, 2s. each.

Our Little Ones.
New and cheaper edition. In elegant cover. Paper boards.

Trimmer's History of the Robins.
24 Illustrations by Harrison Weir. Small 4to, gilt edges.

From Cadet to Captain.
By J. PERCY GROVES. Illustrated by Stanley Berkely.

Friends Though Divided.
A Story of the Cavaliers and Roundheads. By GEORGE HENTY.

Belle's Pink Books.
Sixteen Coloured Plates. By IDA WAUGH.

From May to Christmas at Thorne Hill.
By JOHANNA H. MATTHEWS.

Any Book sent Post Free upon receipt of Stamps to value of Published Price.

The Boys' Own Favourite Library.
Price Three Shillings and Sixpence each.

Under this Title we issue, in one uniform series, a number of the best known and most popular books for boys, written by their favourite authors, such as W. H. G. Kingston, G. A. Henty, Rev. H. C. Adams, Jules Verne, E. Marryat Norris, and others.

The books are well printed in 12mo size on good paper, and strongly and elegantly bound, and will be found the cheapest and best library for boys' reading. Each volume contains from 350 to 500 pages of solid reading, and they are all well illustrated.

Manco.	By W. H. G. Kingston.
Chums.	By Harleigh Severne.
The African Wanderers.	By Mrs Lee.
Tales of the White Cockade.	By Barbara Hutton.
The Three Admirals.	By W. H. G. Kingston.
The Missing Ship.	By W. H. G. Kingston.
Will Weatherhelm.	By W. H. G. Kingston.
The Fiery Cross.	By Barbara Hutton.
Travel, War, & Shipwreck.	By Col. Parker Gillmore.
True Blue.	By W. H. G. Kingston.
The North Pole.	
John Deane.	By W. H. G. Kingston.
College Days at Oxford.	By the Rev. H. C. Adams.
Mark Seaworth.	By W. H. G. Kingston.
Hurricane Hurry.	By W. H. G. Kingston.
Salt Water.	By W. H. G. Kingston.
Out on the Pampas.	By G. A. Henty.
Peter the Whaler.	By W. H. G. Kingston.
Early Start in Life.	By E. Marryat Norris.
Fred Markham in Russia.	By W. H. G. Kingston.
The Three Midshipmen.	By W. H. G. Kingston.
The Three Commanders.	By W. H. G. Kingston.
The Three Lieutenants.	By W. H. G. Kingston.
The Young Francs Tireurs.	By G. A. Henty.
Harty the Wanderer.	By Farleigh Owen.
Our Soldiers.	By W. H. G. Kingston.
Our Sailors.	By W. H. G. Kingston.

A Liberal Discount to the Clergy and the Scholastic Profession.

The Girls' Own Favourite Library.

Price Three Shillings and Sixpence each.

(*Uniform with the Boys' Own Favourite Library.*)

Shiloh.	By W. M. L. Jay.
Holden with the Cords.	By W. M. L. Jay.
Rosamond Fane.	By M. A. C. Lee.
Simplicity and Fascination.	By Anne Beale.
Isabel's Difficulties.	By M. R. Carey.
Millicent & her Cousins.	By Hon. Augusta Bethell.
Aunt Hetty's Will.	By M. M. Pollard.
Silver Linings.	By Mrs Bray.
Theodora.	By E. Marryat Norris.
Alda Graham.	By E. Marryat Norris.
The Court and the Cottage.	By Emma Marshall.
Michaelmas Daisy. A New Story.	By Sarah Doudney.
The New Girl.	By Mrs Gellie.
The Oak Staircase.	By M. and C. Lee.
For a Dream's Sake.	By Mrs A. H. Martin.
Gladys, the Reaper.	By Anne Beale.
Stephen, the Schoolmaster.	By Mrs Gellie (M. E. B.)
My Sister's Keeper.	By Laura M. Lane.
"Bonnie Lesley."	By Mrs Herbert Martin.
Left Alone.	By Francis Carr, Author of "Tried by Fire," &c.
Very Genteel.	By Author of "Mrs Jerningham's Journal."
My Mother's Diamonds.	By Maria J. Greer.
A Wayside Posy.	By Fanny Lablache.

Any Book sent Post Free upon receipt of Stamps to value of Published Price.

Griffith and Farran,

A New Uniform Series of Half=Crown Books.

Cloth elegant, fully illustrated.

African Pets;
  Or, Chats about our Animal Friends in Natal. With a Sketch of Kaffir Life. By F. CLINTON PARRY.

Bunchy ;
  Or, The Children of Scarsbrook Farm. By Miss E. C. PHILLIPS, Author of "St Aubyn's Laddie," &c.

Bryan and Katie.
  By ANNETTE LYSTER. Illustrated by Harry Furniss.

A Daring Voyage across the Atlantic,
  By Two Americans, the Brothers ANDREWS, in a small Boat, the *Nautilus*. The Log of the Voyage by Captain WILLIAM A. ANDREWS, with Introduction and Notes by Dr MACAULAY, Editor of the *Boys' Own Paper.*

Dolly, Dear !
  By MARY E. GELLIE (M. E. B.)

Every Inch a King;
  Or, The Story of Rex and his Friends. By Mrs J. WORTHINGTON BLISS.

"Those Unlucky Twins ! "
  By A. LYSTER.

A Gem of an Aunt.
  By Mrs GELLIE (M. E. B.).

Growing Up :
  A Story of Girls, which Boys may read for all that.

Hilda and Her Doll.
  By E. C. PHILLIPS, Author of " Bunchy," &c.

The House on the Bridge,
  And other Tales. By C. E. BOWEN, Author of " Among the Brigands," &c.

Kitty and Bo;
  Or, The Story of a very little Girl and Boy. By A. T. With Frontispiece.

Nora's Trust ;
  Or, Uncle Ned's Money. By Mrs GELLIE (M. E. B.).

Gerty and May.
  By the Author of "Granny's Story Box."

Punch.
  By Miss E. C. PHILLIPS, Author of "Bunchy."

St Aubyn's Laddie.
  By Miss E. C. PHILLIPS, Author of " Bunchy."

Two Rose Trees :
  The Adventures of Twin Sisters. By Mrs MINNIE DOUGLAS.

Ways and Tricks of Animals,
  With Stories about Aunt Mary's Pets. By MARY HOOPER.

We Four.
  By Mrs R. M. BRAY.

A Liberal Discount to the Clergy and the Scholastic Profession.

St Paul's Churchyard, London.   7

The Cherry Series

For Presents and Prizes for Boys and Girls.

They are all illustrated and attractively bound in cloth, printed in gold and silver.

Price One Shilling and Sixpence each.

Adventures in Fanti-land. By Mrs R. Lee.
Always Happy; or, Anecdotes of Felix and his Sister.
A Child's Influence. By Lisa Lockyer.
Battle and Victory. By C. E. Bowen.
Constance and Nellie. By Emma Davenport.
Corner Cottage, and its Inmates. By Frances Osborne.
Distant Homes. By Mrs J. E. Aylmer.
Father Time's Story Book. By Kathleen Knox.
From Peasant to Prince. By Mrs Pietzker.
Good in Everything. By Mrs Barwell.
Granny's Wonderful Chair. By B. F. Browne.
Happy Holidays. By Emma Davenport.
Happy Home. By Lady Lushington.
The Heroic Wife. By W. H. G. Kingston.
Helen in Switzerland. By Lady Lushington.
Holidays Abroad. By Emma Davenport.
Lucy's Campaign. By M. & C. Lee.
Lost in the Jungle. By Augusta Marryat.
Louisa Broadhurst. By A. Milner.
My Grandmother's Budget. By Mrs Broderip.
Our Birthdays. By Emma Davenport.
Our Home in the Marshland. By E. L. F.
Pictures of Girl Life. By C. A. Howell.
School Days in Paris. By M. S. Le Jeune.

Any Book sent Post Free upon receipt of Stamps to value of Published Price.

The Hawthorn Series

For Presents and Prizes for Boys and Girls.

They are all illustrated and attractively bound in cloth, printed in gold and silver.

Price One Shilling each.

Adrift on the Sea. By E. M. Norris.
Alice and Beatrice. By Grandmamma.
Among the Brigands. By C. E. Bowen.
The Children's Picnic. By E. Marryat Norris.
Christian Elliot; or, Mrs Danver's Prize. By L. N. Comyn.
Claudine. By the Author of "William Tell," &c.
Cat and Dog; or, Puss and the Captain.
Children of the Parsonage.
The Discontented Children. By M. & E. Kirby.
Fickle Flora and her Seaside Friends. By E. Davenport.
Grandmamma's Relics. By C. E. Bowen.
Harry at School. A Story for Boys. By E. Marryat Norris.
The Hero of Brittany.
Hofer, the Tyrolese. By the Author of "William Tell."
Holiday Tales. By Florence Wilford.
Holidays among the Mountains. By M. Betham Edwards.
Johnny Miller. By Felix Weiss.
Julia Maitland. By M. & E. Kirby.
Our White Violet.
Paul Howard's Captivity. By E. Marryat Norris.
The Stolen Cherries; or, Tell the Truth at Once.
Sunny Days.
Wrecked, not Lost. By the Hon. Mrs Dundas.
William Tell, the Patriot of Switzerland. By Florian.

A Liberal Discount to the Clergy and the Scholastic Profession.

St Paul's Churchyard, London.   9

The Holly Series of Toy Books.
Price Sixpence each.

Six different kinds, exquisitely printed in bright colours. Original designs by IDA WAUGH.   Verses by AMY BLANCHARD.

1. *Holly-Gatherers.*
2. *Little May.*
3. *Horatio Hamilton Harris.*
4. *Our Boys.*
5. *Christmas Carol.*
6. *Our Pussy Cat.*

Taking Tales.

Cloth limp, fancy binding, with Chromo on side.
Price Sixpence each.

N.B.—EACH TALE IS ILLUSTRATED AND COMPLETE IN ITSELF, AND VERY SUITABLE FOR VILLAGE LIBRARIES, &c.

1. *The Miller of Hillbrook:* A Rural Tale.
2. *Tom Trueman:* A Sailor in a Merchantman.
3. *Michael Hale and His Family in Canada.*
4. *John Armstrong*, the Soldier.
5. *Joseph Rudge*, the Australian Shepherd.
6. *Life Underground;* or, Dick the Colliery Boy.
7. *Life on the Coast;* or, the Little Fisher Girl.
8. *Adventures of Two Orphans in London.*
9. *Early Days on Board a Man-of-War.*
10. *Walter, the Foundling:* A Tale of Olden Times.
11. *The Tenants of Sunnyside Farm.*
12. *Holmwood;* or, The New Zealand Settler.
13. *A Bit of Fun, and what it cost.*
14. *Sweethearts:* A Tale of Village Life.
15. *Helpful Sam.*
16. *Little Pretty.*
17. *A Wise Woman.*

N.B.—Nos. 1 TO 12 MAY ALSO BE HAD IN 4 VOLS. 1S. 6D. EACH, AND 2 VOLS. 3S. 6D. EACH.

Any Book sent Post Free upon receipt of Stamps to value of Published Price.

Our Boys' and Girls' Little Library.

PICTURES AND READING FOR LITTLE FOLK.

A Series of Twenty-four elegant little volumes in cloth extra, price Sixpence each. Every Page Illustrated.

They are especially suited for School Prizes and Rewards.

BOYS.

1. *Papa's Pretty Gift Book.*
2. *Mamma's Pretty Gift Book.*
3. *Neddy's Picture Story Book.*
4. *Stories for Play Time.*
5. *The Christmas Gift Book.*
6. *The Prize Picture Book.*
7. *Little Tommy's Story Book.*
8. *Bright Picture Pages.*
9. *My Little Boy's Story Book.*
10. *What Santa Claus gave me.*
11. *Tiny Stories for Tiny Boys.*
12. *Little Boy Blue's Picture Book.*

GIRLS.

1. *Nellie's Picture Stories.*
2. *Stories and Pictures for Little Troublesome.*
3. *Little Trotabout's Picture Stories.*
4. *Birdie's Scrap Book.*
5. *Stories for Little Curly Locks.*
6. *Bright Pictures for Roguish Eyes.*
7. *Daisy's Picture Album.*
8. *Wee-Wee Stories for Wee-Wee Girls.*
9. *May's Little Story Book.*
10. *Gipsy's Favourite Companion.*
11. *My Own Story Book.*
12. *Pretty Pet's Gift Book.*

A Liberal Discount to the Clergy and the Scholastic Profession.

Educational Books.

The "Standard Authors" Readers.

ARRANGED AND ANNOTATED BY

The Editor of "Poetry for the Young."

THE Books have been planned throughout to meet exactly the requirements of the New Mundella Code. They are well printed from clear type, on good paper, bound in a strong and serviceable manner, and have *interesting and useful Illustrations from beginning to end.*

In the Infants' Books of the Series, very careful graduation in the introduction of sounds and words is combined with that great desideratum in Infants' Readers—an interesting *connected narrative form.*

The distinctive features of the Series in the Higher Books are that the passages selected (both prose and poetry) are taken from the *Works of Standard Authors*, thus complying with the requirements of the New Code, and that they are of such a nature as to awaken, sustain, and cultivate the interest of youthful readers.

The Explanatory Matter is placed at the end of each book, so that children may, at the discretion of the teacher, be debarred access to it, and takes the form of three Appendices:—

   (*a*) **Explanatory Notes.**   (*b*) **Biographical Notes.**
   (*c*) **A Glossary of Rare or Difficult Words.**

The compilation has been made with the utmost care, with the assistance and advice of gentlemen long conversant with the requirements of Public Elementary Schools; and the Publishers feel that the literary, artistic, and mechanical excellences of the Books are such that the Series will be pronounced

The "Ne Plus Ultra" of School Reading Books.

*** SPECIMEN PAGES AND FULL PROSPECTUSES, WITH TABLES OF CONTENTS OF THE VARIOUS BOOKS, ARE READY FOR DISTRIBUTION TO ALL TEACHERS APPLYING FOR THEM.

LIST OF THE BOOKS IN THE SERIES.

	Price
Primer, Part I., 16 pages, 18 Lessons, 14 Illustrations, paper,	1d.
,, ,, II., 48 ,, 43 ,, 31 ,, ,,	3d.
,, ,, IIA, being the first 32 pages of Primer II., ,,	2d.
Infant Reader, 64 pages, 55 Lessons, 32 Illustrations, cloth,	4d.
,, ,, (abridged) being the 1st 48 pages of Infant Reader, cl.,	3d.
,, ,, (enlarged) ,, Infant Reader increased by 16 pages, cloth,	5d.
Standard I., Reader, 96 pages, 51 Lessons, 29 Illustrations, cloth,	6d.
,, II., ,, 144 ,, 62 ,, 34 ,, ,,	9d.
,, III., ,, 192 ,, 62 ,, 25 ,, ,,	1/-
,, IV., ,, 288 ,, 71 ,, 26 ,, ,,	1/6
,, V., ,, 320 ,, 86 ,, 22 ,, ,,	1/9
,, VI., ,, 384 ,, 92 ,, 25 ,, ,,	2/-

A Liberal Discount to the Clergy and the Scholastic Profession.

Poetical Readers for the Standards.
ILLUSTRATED.
Adopted by the London School Board.

"Poetry for the Young," the most complete collection of high-class Poetry in the English Language, has met with so favourable a reception that we have brought it out in a form and at a price which will place it within the reach of EVERY CHILD IN EVERY SCHOOL.

The choicest Poems in the collection have been selected for the SEPARATE BOOKS for SEPARATE STANDARDS, and the utmost pains have been taken to make the print, paper, and binding as perfect as possible.

The Prices and Sizes of the Books are as follows :—

Book I. for Standard I.	...	16 pp.	...	1d.
" II. "	" II.	...	32 pp.	...	2d.
" III. "	" III.	...	32 pp.	...	2d.
" IV. "	" IV.	...	48 pp.	...	3d.
" V. "	" V.	...	48 pp.	...	3d.
" VI. "	" VI. & VII.	64 pp.	...	4d.

☞ In order to economise space, the *texts* only of the Poems have been given; but the teacher, who possesses the *complete* work, either in one volume or in the four parts, will find everything explained that can possibly need explanation.

Poetry for the Young.
A GRADUATED COLLECTION IN FOUR PARTS.

| Part I. | ... | 128 pp. | ... | 9d. | | Part III. | ... | 194 pp. | ... | 1s. |
| " II. | ... | 176 pp. | ... | 1s. | | " IV. | ... | 166 pp. | ... | 9d. |

Part I. is recommended for the lower Standards; Part II. for the higher; Part III. as a Reading-book (under the New Code) for Standards V., VI., and VII.; and Parts III. and IV. (which can be procured in one volume) as Class-books of Poetry for Candidates and Pupil Teachers.

Poetry for the Young.

The above Collection in One Volume. Fully Illustrated. Crown 8vo, 645 pp., handsomely bound, cloth, price 3s. 6d.; or in Roxburghe binding for presentation, price 5s.

⁎⁎* May also be had in Two Volumes, price 2s. each.

"We cannot too highly recommend the care, the discrimination, and the sound taste that have presided over the selection of this volume of 'Poetry for the Young.'" —*Standard.*

"It is the first successful effort to produce a really well graduated book of poetry for the young."—*Schoolmistress.*

Send for Prospectuses, containing Tables of Contents, &c.

A Liberal Discount to the Clergy and the Scholastic Profession.

St Paul's Churchyard, London.   15

Geographical Readers.

By J. R. BLAKISTON, M.A.

Accepted by the School Boards for Birmingham, Derby, Leeds, London, Leicester, &c.

BOOK I., for STANDARD I.   Price 6d.
Early Glimpses.
Fcap. 8vo, 96 pages, with 22 Illustrations, cloth limp, cut flush.
"This book is largely used in Infant Schools, as an alternative reading book by the First Class. Its use assists in the instruction necessary on the Phenomena of Nature; it contains, amongst other matter, lessons on Vapour, Damp, Dew, Fog, Clouds, Springs, Frost, Water, Wind, Brooks, the Sea, the Pond, Ice, the Tide."

BOOK II., for STANDARD II.   Price 1s.
Glimpses of the Globe.
A Geographical Reading Book.   40 Chapters.   156 pages, cloth.
"A very commendable attempt to simplify the teaching of the elements of geography."—*Educational News.*
"We are strongly of opinion that Mr Blakiston has succeeded most admirably in carrying out his intention in producing this little treatise."—*Educational Chronicle.*

BOOK III., for STANDARD III.   Price 1s.
Glimpses of England.
40 Chapters.   156 pp., cloth.
"Well within the comprehension of Third Standard children, and the book is unquestionably written in pleasant and interesting style."—*Teacher.*

BOOK IV., for STANDARD IV.   Price 1s. 6d.
Glimpses of the British Empire.
In 66 Sections.   Cloth.
"The whole volume contains a very fair outline of the empire on which the sun never sets."—*School.*
"This little volume should be specially noted by teachers in search of a good geographical reading book."—*Educational Times.*

BOOK V., for STANDARDS V.–VII.   Price 2s. 6d.
Glimpses of the Earth.
320 pages, cloth.
"The book is admirably adapted to remind a teacher of the topics he ought to introduce in each lesson."—*Bookseller.*

Exercises in "English,"

Including Questions in Analysis, Parsing, Grammar, Spelling, Prefixes, Suffixes, Wordbuilding, &c.

By HENRY ULLYETT, B.Sc.,
St Mary's School, Folkestone.

These Cards are supplied in Packets of 30 Cards each. Standard VII. has 24. They are provided for Standards II., III., IV., V., VI., VII., price 1s. each. The whole series is expressly prepared to meet the requirements of the Mundella Code.

Any Book sent Post Free upon receipt of Stamps to value of Published Price.

Needlework Manuals and Appliances.

Sectional Paper,
For use with the Diagrams. 9d. per quire.

Chequered Boards
For Needlework Class Teaching Cutting-out, measuring 45 by 36 inches. Chequered in squares of one inch, and a red line at every ninth inch. Price One Guinea.

Lined Paper,
For "Extensions," 36 by 45 inches. 1s. per quire.

Threaders,
5d. per 100; postage 4d. extra.

Plain Hints
For those who have to examine Needlework, whether for Government Grants, Prize Associations, or Local Managers; to which is added Skeleton Demonstration Lessons to be used with the Demonstration Frames, and a Glossary of terms used in the Needlework required from the Scholars in Public Elementary Schools. By the same Author. Price 2s.

Needlework,
Schedule III., exemplified and illustrated. By Mrs E. A. Curtis. Eighth thousand. Cloth, 30 illustrations, 1s.

The Demonstration Frame,
For Class Teaching, on which the formation of almost any Stitch may be exhibited, is used in the best German schools. Complete with special Needle and Cord. Price 5s. 6d.

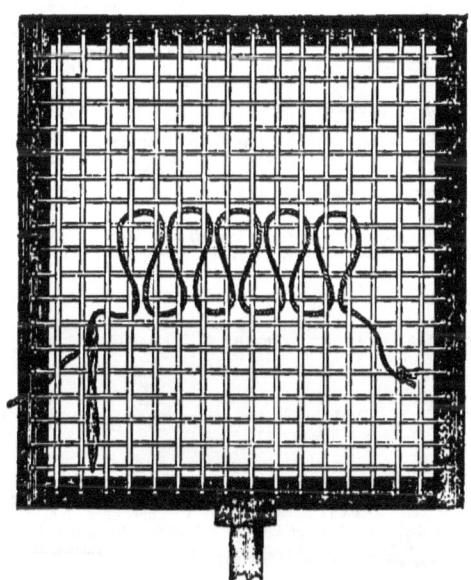

Any Book sent Post Free on receipt of Stamps to value of Published Price.

Needlework Class Teaching.
RECOMMENDED BY THE EDUCATION DEPARTMENT.

They contain full instructions as to PIN DRILL, POSITION DRILL, *and* NEEDLE DRILL, *as required by the New Code.*

Needle Drill, Position Drill, Pin Drill, Thimble Drill. Price 3d.

Needlework Demonstration Sheets
(Nineteen in number). Exhibiting by Diagrams and Descriptions the formation of the stitches in Elementary needlework. 30 by 22 inches, price 9d. each; or mounted on rollers and varnished, 2s. 6d.

THE FOLLOWING IS A LIST OF THE SERIES, WHICH IS NOW COMPLETE :—

Alphabets for Marking	6 Sheets.	Button Hole	.	1 Sheet.
True Marking Stitch .	1 Sheet.	Whip Stitch for Frills, and		
Herring Bone . . .	1 "	Fern or Coral Stitch	.	1 "
Fisherman's Stitch for		Hemming, Seaming, and		
Braiding Nets . .	1 "	Stitching . . .	.	1 "
Stocking Web Stitch		Knots, Shortening Knots,		
(Darning) . . .	1 "	Slip Knots, Joining Knots	1	"
Grafting Stocking Material	1 "	Stocking Sheet . .	.	1 "
Setting in Gathers, or		Invariable Stocking Scale	1	"
Stocking, Knotting, or		Swiss Darning . .	.	1 "
Seeding (*English Method*) .	1 "			

Plain Needlework,
Arranged in Six Standards, with Hints for the Management of Classes, and Appendix on Simultaneous Teaching. By Mrs A. FLOYER, Principal of the London Institute for Plain Needlework, late Senior Examiner of Needlework to the London School Board. Twenty-third thousand. Sewed, 6d.

Plain Knitting and Mending,
Arranged in Six Standards, with Diagrams. Sixteenth thousand. By the Same. 6d.

Plain Cutting-Out,
For Standards IV., V., VI., as now required by the Government Educational Department. Adapted to the Principles of Elementary Geometry. By the same. Sewed, 1s.

The Diagrams,
Referred to in the Book, printed on stout paper and enclosed in an envelope. Price 1s.

Drawing Book,
Needlework Schedule III., Educational Code for 1882. Cutting-out required in Standards V., VI., and VII., and for Pupil Teachers of the fourth year. Containing also copies of Schedule III. for Girls, the Schedule for Pupil Teachers, and the instruction to Her Majesty's Inspectors. Appendix I., Needlework on the day of Inspection. Price 3d.

A Liberal Discount to the Clergy and the Scholastic Profession.

George Darnell's Copy-Books.

After over a quarter of a century of public favour, are everywhere acknowledged as the best for simplicity and thoroughness. With these Copy-books the pupil advances in the art of writing with ease and rapidity, while the labour of the teacher is very greatly lightened. They are used in nearly all the best schools in Great Britain and the Colonies, and are adapted to the new Educational Code.

ADVANTAGES OF THE SYSTEM.

I. It is the production of an experienced Schoolmaster.
II. It gradually advances from the Simple Stroke to a superior Small-hand.
III. The assistance given in the primal lesson is reduced as the learner progresses, until all guidance is safely withdrawn.
IV. The number and variety of the copies secure attention, and prevent the pupils copying their own writing, as in books with single headlines.
V. The system insures the progress of the learner, and greatly lightens the labours of the teacher.

Darnell's Universal Twopenny Copy-books,

for the Standards. 16 Nos., Fcap. 4to.

STANDARD I.
1. Elementary.
2. Single and Double Letters.
3. Large Text (Short Words).

STANDARD II.
3. Large Text (Short Words).
4. Large Text (Short Words).
5. Text, Large Text, and Figures.

STANDARD III.
6. Text, Round, Capitals and Figures.
7. Text, Round and Small.
8. Text, Round, Small, and Figures.

STANDARD IV.
9. Text, Round, Small, and Figures.
10. Text, Round, Small, and Figures.
11. Round, Small, and Figures.

STANDARD V.
12. Round, Small, and Figures.
13. Round and Small.
14. Round and Small.

STANDARD VI.
15. Small Hand.
16. Small Hand.

Darnell's Large Post Copy-books.

A sure and certain road to a good handwriting. 16 Nos., 6d. each. Being a series of Sixteen copy-books, by GEORGE DARNELL, the first ten of which have on every alternate line appropriate and carefully-written copies, in Pencil-coloured Ink, to be first written over, and then imitated; the remaining numbers having Black Headlines for imitation only. *The whole gradually advancing from a Simple Stroke to a superior Small-hand.*

No.
1 Elementary (Strokes, &c.)
2 Single Letters.
3, 4 Large Text (Short Words).
5 Text, Large Text, and Figures.
6 Round Text, Capitals, and Figures.

No.
7 Text, Round, and Small.
8, 9, 10 Text, Round, Small, and Figures.
11, 12 Round, Small, and Figures.
13, 14 Round and Small.
15, 16 Small-hand.

Darnell's Foolscap Copy-books.

A sure guide to a good handwriting, on the same plan. 24 Nos., 3d. each, green covers; or on a superior paper, marble covers, 4d. each.

No.
1 Elementary (Strokes, &c.)
2 Single Letters.
3, 4 Large Text (Short Words).
5 Text, Large Text, and Figures.
6 Text, Round, and Capitals.
Round, Small, and Figures.
Text, Round, and Small.

No.
9 Round, Small, and Figures.
10, 11 Round and Small.
12, 13, 15 Round, Small, and Figures.
14 Round and Small.
16 to 20 Small hand.
21 Ornamental Hands.
22 to 24 Ladies' Angular Writing.

Any Book sent Post Free upon receipt of Stamps to value of Published Price.

Devotional and Religious Books.

Devotional and Religious Books.

An Epitome of Anglican Church History
From the Earliest Ages to the Present Time. Compiled from various sources by ELLEN WEBLEY-PARRY. Demy 8vo, cloth, 7s. 6d.

The Life Militant.
Plain Sermons for Cottage Homes. By ELLELI. Crown 8vo, price 6s.

The Way of Prayer;
A Book of Devotions, for use in Church and at Home. Compiled by Rev. H. W. MILLAR, M.A. Cloth, red edges, 1s.

Confirmation;
Or, Called and Chosen and Faithful. By the author of "The Gospel in the Church's Seasons" Series. With Preface by the Very Rev. the DEAN OF CHESTER. Fcap. 8vo., cloth limp. 1s.
A Cheaper Edition for Distribution, price 9d.

HANDSOME PRESENT FOR A CHURCH.

Dr Lee's Altar Services.
Edited by the Rev. Dr. F. G. LEE, D.C.L., F.S.A. Containing the complete Altar Services of the Church, beautifully printed in red and black at the Chiswick Press, enriched with Ornamental Capitals, &c., in three volumes; one volume, folio size, 15 × 10 × 1½ inches; and two volumes 4to, containing the Epistles and Gospels separately, each 12 × 9 × ¾ inches.

The Set, in Turkey Morocco, plain,	£7	7 0
Do. Best Levant Morocco, inlaid cross,	10	10 0

The Folio Volume, which contains all the Services of the Altar, may be had separately—

Turkey Morocco, plain,	£3	3 0
Best Levant Morocco, inlaid cross,	4	4 0

₄ The work can also be bound specially to order in cheaper or more expensive styles.

Messrs GRIFFITH & FARRAN have a few copies remaining of this rare and valuable work, which is not only the best book for the purpose for which it is designed, but is one of the finest specimens of typographical art which the Chiswick Press has produced.

A few copies in Vellum, 30s. the 3 vols.

Parish Work:
A Book of Parochial Theory and Practice, by the Rev. EDWARD COLLETT, Vicar of Bowerchalk. Price 5s.

Any Book sent Post Free upon receipt of Stamps to value of Published Price.

Sermons for Children.
    Translated from the French of A. DECOPPET by MARIE TAYLOR. With an Introduction by Mrs HENRY REEVES. Small crown 8vo., cloth, 3s. 6d.

A Catechism of Church Doctrine
    For Younger Children. By Rev. T. S. HALL, M.A. Price 1d.; or cloth, 2d.

Whispers of Love and Wisdom.
    By ANNE CAZENOVE. Price 6d.; or leather, 1s. 2d.

Fragments in Prose and Verse.
    By same Author. Uniform in price and size with above.

Cut Diamonds.
    By Mrs GUBBINS. Uniform in price and size with above.

The above three Books may be had in Cloth Case, 2s.; or Leather, 3s. 6d.

The Children's Daily Help
    For the Christian Year. Selected from the Psalms. By E. G. Price 1s. 6d. Gilt edges, 2s.

Daily Thoughts of Comfort.
    Text and Verse, in large type. By E. G. Price 3s. 6d.

Bogatzky's Golden Treasury.
    Cloth, plain, 1s.; gilt edges, 1s. 6d.

Private Prayers.
    In large type, 1d.; cloth 3d.

Introits for the Church's Seasons,
    And for Special Occasions. Price 1d.: or cloth, 2d.

A Liberal Discount to the Clergy and the Scholastic Profession.

Altar Manuals, etc.

The Churchman's Altar Manual and Guide
to Holy Communion.

Together with the Collects, Epistles, and Gospels, and a selection of appropriate Hymns. Borders and Rubrics in red.

Three Editions of this Manual are now issued. The following are the sizes and prices:—

Royal 32mo, with Rubrics and Borders in red, cloth, 2s., or with Eight Photos, 4s. (a Confirmation Card is presented with this edition).

Large Type Edition, cloth, red edges, 2s.

Cheap Edition, for distribution, cloth flush, 6d.; or red edges, 9d.

FOR THE USE OF NEWLY-CONFIRMED AND OTHERS.

The Young Communicant's Manual.

Containing Instructions and Preparatory Prayers in accordance with the Church's directions for Preparations; Form of Self-Examination; the Services for the Holy Communion, with appropriate Devotions, Intercessions, and Thanksgivings; Hymns, &c. Price 1s.

Ken's Approach to the Holy Altar.

With an Address to Young Communicants. New and Cheaper Edition. Limp cloth, 8d.; superior cloth, red edges, 1s.; or with Photographs, 4s.

The Churchman's Manual of Family and
Private Devotion.

Compiled from the Writings of English Divines, with Graces and Devotions for the Seasons, Litanies, and an entirely new selection of Hymns. Super Royal 32mo, price 1s. 6d. Bevelled boards, red edges, 2s.

⁂ All the above may be had in various styles of leather bindings.

Any Book sent Post Free upon receipt of Stamps to value of Published Price.

American Sermons and Theological Books

PUBLISHED BY

E. P. DUTTON & CO., NEW YORK, U.S.A.,

AND SOLD IN ENGLAND BY

GRIFFITH AND FARRAN.

Brooks, the Rev. Phillips, D.D., Rector of Trinity Church, Boston.
    Influence of Jesus. Being the Bohlen Lecture for 1879. Eighth Thousand. Crown 8vo, cloth, price 3s. 6d.
    Sermons. Thirteenth Thousand. Crown 8vo, cloth, price 5s.

Chapman, Rev. Dr.
    Sermons upon the Ministry, Worship, and Doctrine of the Church. New Edition. Crown 8vo, price 5s.
    Clergyman's Visiting List, in morocco, with tuck for the pocket. Foolscap, price 7s. 6d.

Doane, Right Rev. William Croswell, D.D., Bishop of Albany.
    Mosaics; or, The Harmony of Collect, Epistle, and Gospel for the Sundays of the Christian Year. Crown 8vo, cloth, 6s.

Hallam, Rev. Robert A., D.D.
    Lectures on the Morning Prayer. 12mo, 5s.
    Lectures on Moses. 12mo, cloth, 3s. 6d.

Handbook of Church Terms.
    A Pocket Dictionary; or, Brief Explanation of Words in Common Use relating to the Order, Worship, Architecture, Vestments, Usages, and Symbolism of the Church, as employed in Christian Art. Paper, 9d.; cloth, 1s. 6d.

Hobart, Rev. John Henry, D.D., formerly Bishop of New York.
    Festivals and Fasts. A Companion for the Festivals and Fasts of the Protestant Episcopal Church, principally selected and altered from Nelson's Companion. With Forms of Devotion. Twenty-third Edition. 12mo, 5s.

Hodges, Rev. William, D.D.
    Baptism: Tested by Scripture and History; or, The Teaching of the Holy Scriptures, and the Practice and Teaching of the Christian Church in every age succeeding the Apostolic, compared in relation to the subjects and Modes of Baptism. 6s.

Huntington, Right Rev. F. D., Bishop of Central New York.
    Christian Believing and Living. Sermons. Fifth Edition. 12mo., 3s. 6d.
    Helps to a Holy Lent. 16mo, 208 pages, crown 8vo, 2s. 6d.
    Sermons for the People. Crown 8vo, cloth, 3s. 6d.

Odenheimer, Rt. Rev. Wm. H., D.D., late Bishop of New Jersey.
    Sermons, with Portrait and Memoir. Edited by his Wife. Crown 8vo, 5s.

Staunton, Rev. William, D.D.
    Ecclesiastical Dictionary, containing Definitions of Terms, and Explanations and Illustrations of Subjects pertaining to the History, Ritual, Discipline, Worship, Ceremonies, and Usages of the Christian Church. 8vo, 746 pages, 7s. 6d.

Vinton, Rev. Alexander H.
    Sermons. Fourth Edition. 330 pages, 3s. 6d.

Vinton, Francis, S.T.D., D.C.L.
    Manual Commentary on the General Canon Law of the Protestant Episcopal Church. 8vo, cloth, 5s.

Williams, Right Rev. John, D.D., Bishop of Connecticut.
    Studies on the English Reformation. 12mo, cloth, 3s. 6d.

Wilson, Rev. William D., D.D.
    The Church Identified. By a reference to the History of its Origin, Extension, and Perpetuation, with Special Reference to the Protestant Episcopal Church in the United States. Revised Edition. 12mo, 439 pages, 6s.

A Liberal Discount to the Clergy and the Scholastic Profession.

St Paul's Churchyard, London.

Holy Bibles. For Lectern Use.
Containing the Apocrypha.

Large size, $13 \times 11 \times 4$.
Turkey morocco, plain, from 50s.

Smaller size, $11\frac{1}{2} \times 9\frac{1}{2} \times 3\frac{1}{2}$.
Turkey morocco, plain, from 30s.
Family Bibles from One Guinea each.

Holy Bibles, Without References.

Small Pica 8vo, $9\frac{1}{4} \times 5\frac{3}{4} \times 2$.
Cloth, red edges, 4s. 6d. | French morocco, 7s. 6d.
Turkey morocco, 12s. 6d.

Brevier 16mo, $6\frac{3}{4} \times 4\frac{3}{4} \times 2$.
Cloth, red edges, 4s. | French morocco, 4s. 6d.
Turkey morocco.

Pearl 24mo, $5\frac{3}{8} \times 3\frac{1}{4} \times 1$.
Cloth, red edges, 1s. | French morocco, 1s. 6d.
Smooth calf, 4s. 6d.
With Sepia Plates, from 1s. 6d. each.

Holy Bibles, With References.

Minion 8vo, $8 \times 5\frac{1}{2} \times 1\frac{1}{3}$.
Cloth, red edges, 5s. 6d. | French morocco, 7s. 6d.
Turkey morocco, 12s. 6d.

Nonpariel 8vo, $7 \times 4\frac{3}{4} \times 1\frac{1}{4}$.
Cloth, red edges, 3s. 6d. | French morocco, 4s. 6d.
Turkey morocco, 7s. 6d.

Ruby 16mo, $6\frac{1}{2} \times 4\frac{1}{8} \times 1\frac{1}{8}$.
Cloth, red edges, 3s. | French morocco, 3s. 6d.
Turkey morocco, 6s.

Pearl 16mo, $5\frac{1}{2} \times 4 \times 1\frac{1}{8}$.
Cloth, red edges, 2s. | French morocco, 3s.
Turkey morocco, 5s.

Most of the above may be had with Apocrypha from 1s. 6d. each extra, with flap edges, from 2s. each extra.

Any Book sent Post Free upon receipt of Stamps to value of Published Price.

Common Prayers bound up with Hymns Ancient and Modern.

Bourgeois 24mo, $5\frac{1}{2} \times 4 \times 1\frac{1}{2}$.

Cloth, red edges, 2s. 6d.	Smooth calf, 6s. 6d.
French morocco, 3s. 6d.	Morocco, 6s. 6d.

Minion 32mo, $4\frac{1}{2} \times 3 \times 1\frac{1}{8}$.

French morocco, 2s. 6d.
    Ditto,   2 volumes in case, 5s.
Calf or morocco, 4s.
    Ditto,   2 volumes in case, 8s. 6d.

Nonpariel 32mo, $5 \times 3\frac{1}{4} \times \frac{3}{4}$.

French morocco, 2s.	Calf or morocco, 4s.
Persian calf, 2s. 6d.	Russia, flap edges, 7s.

Ruby 32mo, $4 \times 3 \times 1$.

French morocco, 1s.	Calf or morocco, 2s. 6d.

Calf or morocco, 2 volumes in case, 8s. 6d.
Russia, flap edges, 4s. 6d.

Diamond 48mo, $3\frac{3}{4} \times 2\frac{1}{2} \times 1$.

French morocco, 1s. 6d.	Smooth calf, 3s.
Persian, flap edges, 2s. 6d.	Russia, flap edges, 4s. 6d.

Most of the above sizes are issued with rubrics in red, at a small extra cost.

COMMON PRAYERS are also kept bound up with Church Hymns and Hymnal Companion, at similar prices to above.

Any Book sent Post Free upon receipt of Stamps to value of Published Price.

St Paul's Churchyard, London. 27

Common Prayers.

Pica 16mo, *square large type*, $7\frac{3}{8} \times 5\frac{5}{8} \times \frac{3}{4}$.

Cloth, red edges, 2s. 6d. | French morocco, 3s. 6d.
Persian calf, 5s. | Turkey morocco, 7s. 6d.

Small Pica 16mo, $7 \times 4\frac{1}{2} \times \frac{3}{4}$.

Cloth, red edges, 2s. 6d. | French morocco, 3s. 6d.
Calf or Turkey morocco, 6s. | Morocco, flap edges, 9s.

Long Primer 24mo, $5\frac{1}{2} \times 3\frac{1}{4} \times \frac{7}{8}$.

Cloth, red edges, 1s. 6d. | French morocco, 2s.
Smooth calf, 4s. 6d. | Morocco flaps, 6s. 6d.

Bourgeois 32mo, $5 \times 3\frac{1}{8} \times \frac{3}{4}$.

French morocco, 1s. | Smooth calf, 3s. 6d.
Morocco, flap edges, 5s. | Russia limp, 5s.

Minion 32mo, $4\frac{1}{2} \times 2\frac{5}{8} \times \frac{5}{8}$.

Cloth, red edges, 1s. | Persian calf, 1s. 8d.
French morocco, 1s. 6d. | Smooth calf, 3s.

Ruby 32mo, $4\frac{1}{2} \times 3 \times \frac{3}{8}$.

French morocco, 9d. | Calf or morocco, 2s. 6d.
Russia flap edges, 4s.

Ruby 48mo, $3\frac{7}{8} \times 2\frac{5}{8} \times \frac{1}{2}$.

Leatherette, 6d. | French morocco, 1s.
Calf or morocco, 1s. 6d. | Morocco flap edges, 3s. 6d.

Diamond 48mo, $3\frac{3}{4} \times 2\frac{1}{4} \times \frac{3}{8}$.

French morocco, 9d. | Persian, flap edges, 1s. 6d.
Calf or morocco, 1s. 6d. | Russia, flap edges, 3s.

Most of the above sizes are issued with rubrics in red, at a small extra cost.

A Liberal Discount to the Clergy and the Scholastic Profession.

Miscellaneous Books,
In best quality leather bindings.

The Christian Year.
Small size, French morocco, 1s. 6d.
Second size,   ,,   3s. 6d.
Large size,   ,,   6s.

Imitation of Christ.
Small size, French morocco, 1s. 6d.
Second size,   ,,   1s. 6d.
Large size, morocco limp, 10s.

Benedicite.
Tree calf, 12s. 6d.

Treasury of Devotion.
French morocco, 3s. 6d.
Calf or morocco, 5s.

Cruden's Concordance.
French morocco, 3s. 6d.

Daily Round, The.
32mo, French morocco, 4s.
,, smooth calf, 6s.
Also three sizes larger in various styles.

Gold Dust.
Two parts in one. French morocco, 2s. 6d.
Smooth calf, 3s. 6d.

Havergal's My King, &c.
Six vols., French morocco, each 2s.

Havergal's Under the Surface, &c.
Three vols., each 2s.

Havergal's Life Mosaic.
French morocco, 16s.
Morocco antique, 25s.

Havergal's Life Chords and Swiss Letters.
Uniform with "Life Mosaic" in size and price.

A Liberal Discount to the Clergy and the Scholastic Profession.

St Paul's Churchyard, London. 29

Miscellaneous Books,
In best quality leather bindings.

Farrar's Life of Christ.
Crown 8vo, half Persian, 9s.
  „   morocco antique, 13s. 6d.

Smiles' Self-Help, Character, Thrift, and Duty.
Tree calf, each 12s. 6d.

Lyra Innocentium.
18mo, French morocco, 5s.
  „   smooth calf, 7s. 6d.

Macaulay's Lays of Ancient Rome.
Small Edition, French morocco, 2s. 6d.
  „   smooth calf, 5s.

Narrow Way, The.
Small size, French morocco, 1s. 4d.
  „   smooth calf, 2s. 6d.

Taylor's Holy Living.
18mo, French morocco, 2s. 6d.

Taylor's Holy Dying.
18mo, French morocco, 2s. 6d.

Taylor's Holy Living and Dying.
Two vols. in one, 18mo, French morocco, 3s. 6d.

Tennyson's Poetical Works.
1 vol. crown 8vo, Persian, 10s. 6d.
  „   „   morocco, 12s. 6d.
With Photos., 6s. extra.

Standard Poets.
Red line edition, all the most popular Authors, Persian, 6s.
Larger edition, Persian, 8s. 6d.

Shakespeare's Works.
Miniature edition, 12 vols. in neat box, French morocco, 25s.
Turkey morocco, 50s.

Any Book sent Post Free upon receipt of Stamps to value of Published Price.

Common Prayer, with Hymns, Ancient and Modern.

The Royal.   TWO VOLS. IN CASE.

Contains the Diamond 48mo size Prayer and Hymns, in best smooth calf, with floral design hand-painted on each book, nickel lock and handle, price 12s. 6d.

The Princess.   TWO VOLS. IN CASE.

Similar Books to above, different shape case, with plain books, 12s. 6d.

Either of the above Cases may be had in various sizes and styles of bindings.

A Liberal Discount to the Clergy and the Scholastic Profession.

Birthday Books.

The Anniversary Text-Book.
Quotations from Scripture, with blank spaces for writing.

| Cloth, plain, 1s. | French morocco, 2s. |
| Cloth, gilt edges, 1s. 6d. | Calf or moroco, 4s. |

The Book of Remembrance.
Choice Extracts from Popular Authors.
Printed in red and black.

| Cloth, plain, 2s. | French morocco, 3s. 6d. |
| Cloth, gilt edges, 2s. 6d. | Calf or morocco, 5s. |

The Churchman's Daily Remembrancer.
Text and Verse for every Day in the Year.
Printed in red and black.

Cloth, red edges, 2s. | French morocco, 3s. 6d.
Calf or morocco limp, 4s. 6d.

The Churchman's Birthday Book.
Selections from A' Kempis.

| Cloth, plain, 1s. 6d. | French morocco, 2s. 6d. |
| Cloth, gilt edges, 2s. | Calf or morocco, 4s. 6d. |

The Favourite Birthday Book.
Choice Extracts from Standard Authors.

| Cloth, plain, 6d. | French morocco, 1s. 6d. |
| Cloth, gilt edges, 1s. | Calf limp, 3s. |

The Shakspeare Birthday Book.

Cloth, gilt edges, 2s. 6d. | French morocco, 3s.
Calf or morocco, 5s.

TENNYSON, SCOTT, BURNS, BYRON BIRTHDAY BOOKS,
uniform with Shakspeare in price and size.

Any Book sent Post Free upon receipt of Stamps to value of Published Price.

The Church Hymnal.

NEW EDITION, CONTAINING 475 HYMNS.

*Published by the
Association for Promoting Christian Knowledge, Dublin.*

The following are the sizes published—

Ruby 32mo.

Paper, 1d. | Cloth limp, 2d.

Medium 32mo.

Cloth limp, 6d. | French morocco limp, 1s. 6d.
Cloth, red edges, 8d. | Calf or morocco limp, 3s.

Royal 32mo.

Cloth, 10d. | French morocco, 1s. 9d.

Royal 18mo.

Cloth, red edges, 1s. 4d. | Calf or morocco limp, 5s.
French morocco, 2s. 6d. | Morocco, flap edges, 7s. 6d.

Foolscap 8vo.

Cloth, red edges, 2s. | Calf or morocco, 6s.
French morocco, 3s. 6d. | Morocco, flap edges, 8s.

With Tunes, full score, crown 8vo.

Cloth, red edges, 3s. | French morocco, 6s. 6d.

With Tunes, Organ Edition, 4to.

Cloth, red edges, 7s. 6d.

NEW AND ENLARGED EDITION OF

Chants, Ancient and Modern, Responses, etc.

EDITED BY

SIR ROBERT PRESCOTT STEWART, Mus. D.

This Edition contains 300 Chants, Single and Double, 50 Responses to the Commandments, 22 Doxologies, &c., together with a Biographical Index of Composers.

Small Quarto, paper cover, 2s.
Do., cloth, bevelled boards, red edges, 3s.
Voice Part, 8vo, Canto and Alto, cloth, 1s.
Do., Tenor and Bass, 1s.

A Liberal Discount to the Clergy and the Scholastic Profession.

www.ingramcontent.com/pod-product-compliance
Lightning Source LLC
Chambersburg PA
CBHW030007240426
43672CB00007B/858